A FAMILY
OF
SICILIANS

STORIES AND POEMS

SALVATORE AMICO M. BUTTACI

Publisher:
Salvatore Buttaci
Princeton, West Virginia

Salvatore Buttaci

READ WHAT HAPPENS WHEN...

Crazy old Uncle Tanoots works his best miracle since healing four sick pigs in San Cataldo, Sicily...

A spirit from the next world visits Grandma and asks her to help save a life...

A Sicilian nobleman marches off to war, leaving behind his wife and her two sisters walled up safely in his castle tower...

Grandpa asks his brother-in-law Vincinzu to get his donkey back...

A man accused of murder hires a lawyer who has nothing to say...

A Sicilian bricklayer comes back from the dead to appear live on the *Jay Leno Show* with a message for the world...

The author interviews the real Archimedes whom he has tracked down on the Internet...

A ten-year-old boy in 1900 time-travels to a Benito Mussolini rally in 1922...

AND MORE!

Some of the stories and poems in this collection first
appeared in the following publications:
Buon Giorno! Magazine;   *Daybreak*;   *Sicilia Parra*;
Via: The Voice of the Italian-American;
The Greenwich Village Gazette; *The Manhattanite*;
Poetrymagazine.com; and *Writer's By-Line*.

The poem "Sicily" was published in *Italo-American
Poets: A Bilingual Anthology* [Dr. Ferdinando Alfonsi,
Editor; Cantanzaro, Italy: Antonio Carello Editore,
1985.]

ISBN 0-917398-21-1

Library of Congress Catalog Card Number: 98-96208
Printed in the United States of America.

for
James Presto
(1926-1997)

DADDY

Thank you for your love,
Unconditional day and night
For Saturday matinees
Of Cinderella and Snow White.

For raking the leaves
With me underfoot,
For speaking your mind
No matter how the words were put.

Teaching me to be cautious
Of who gains my trust
For constantly working hard,
But making vacations a must.

For my love of animals
And respect of this earth.
For putting music in my soul,
And giving me self worth.

For the many memories I have
That I will always cherish,
Of a father so grand
Whose love will never perish.
I love you forever...

CONTENTS

SHORT STORIES

INTRODUCTION

This is more than a book of true stories, poems, and short stories. It is a statement of my intense love of all things Sicilian, which motivated me to present a truer image of Sicilians and Sicilian-Americans than the stereotypical mobster image promoted by the media for over two hundred years.

We Sicilian-Americans ought to feel ethnic pride without embarrassment or shame. Most of us are law-abiding citizens who believe in God, family, and country. We need to be proud of our roots and not try to conceal them.

I wrote this book for non-Sicilian-Americans as well, in the hope that they will be persuaded to think more favorably about us, put aside media hype and gross generalizations, and see us as we are. I tried to present this positive image with enough stories and poems to make readers laugh and cry and enjoy themselves.

I would like to thank all those people who encouraged me to write this book, especially my wife Sharon who was there for me with editorial suggestions and much love; my mother and late father for always taking the time to read and praise my work; my brother Alphonse for proofreading my Sicilian; my sisters Anna, Joan, Sarah, and Betty; and a special thanks to my good friend Robert Scussel for his assistance in helping me promote this book.

And I thank you, the reader, for whom I wrote *A Family of Sicilians: Stories and Poems.*

--Salvatore Amico M. Buttaci

TRUE STORIES

"Once a befo' I live in Jersey Cit'," said the old man. "I was a shoemake'. I live a dere ten year."

from: "Somebody to Talk To"

IR' E BENIRI

To travel by bus from Acquaviva Platani, the small Sicilian mountain village of my parents, to the province seat of Caltanissetta requires about two and half hours. The first time I made that trip was back in November 1965 after being in Sicily for only a month. I knew next to nothing of Sicilian or Italian, tried to get by with some simple sign language I hoped would be understood, and I smiled a lot to show the relatives I was happy despite my inability to converse with them.

Most of my time I spent visiting relatives' homes. I'd walk down the cobblestoned streets and I'd hear one of them call out, "*Sarbaturi, trasi. Pigghiamu na tazza di cafè*! [Salvatore, come in. Let's have a cup of coffee!"] Or they'd invite me in for a shot glass of Amaro Siciliano, a favorite bitters apertif. When dinner time came, I found myself invited to this or that cousin's house where I usually ate too much but the laughs were good—usually on me since I didn't understand very much of the conversation—and the company was wonderful.

One morning I got up early, walked four

blocks down Via Vittorio Emanuele and waited by the post office for the bus to Caltanissetta where Zi Nofriu Pitonzo's brother Giuvanni lived with his wife and three sons, as well as did my first cousin Toto Amico, his wife Crocetta and their daughter Lia.

Finally the blue bus arrived as Zi Cicciu predicted: fifteen minutes late. I boarded, found an empty seat, then waited for the ticket conductor.

It was the first time I had seen Peppi Rais, though in that year in Acquaviva, I rode the blue bus quite frequently and as I learned to speak the language, Peppi and I got to be friends. I don't know what his last name was, but everyone called him Peppi "Rais," after "Punto Rais," the airport in Palermo because in the old days, before he was the ticket conductor on the blue Caltanissetta bus, he was the ticket conductor on the blue Palermo bus. He was very short, dark-complexioned, had wavy hair that looked as if someone had painted it pitch-black, then, finding it too dark, tried to cover it with streaks of snow-white. He had few dark teeth despite his forty-something years and whenever he spoke, the words whistled out of his mouth in one of the loudest, deepest voices I'd ever heard.

"*Unni vai?* [Where are you going?"] Peppi

hollers.

"Caltanissetta," I tell him loudly, thinking maybe he's hard of hearing.

"*Ir' e beniri?* [Roundtrip?"] he yells.

"No, Caltanissetta," I explain.

"*Ir' e beniri?*" Peppi yells again.

Now I know he can't hear well so I repeat as loudly and slowly as I can, a syllable at a time: "Cal-ta-ni -sse-tta."

"*Ir' e beniri?*" Peppi still insists.

Can this be happening to me? I wonder. I'm in a rickety old blue-paint-peeling, smoke-chugging, early 20th-Century bus with tires probably bald as eagles that's taking hairpin, rollercoaster turns along the edge of very steep Sicilian mountains while a deaf ticket conductor refuses to sell me a ticket to Caltanissetta, the only destination I want and intend to settle for, so I repeat it still once again: "CALTANISSETTA."

"*'U sacciu!*" ["I know!"] he screams, throwing his hands up in the air like a man possessed. "*IR' E BENIRI?*"

The muscles in my face start to quiver, my eyes twitch, my lips tremble. I can feel the hot air of my patience steaming off me. "Caltanissetta! No *iri beniri!"*

"*Iri sulu?*" ["One way only?"] Peppi Rais asks, for the first time now, smiling.

But I still don't understand; I think he's trying to irritate me a little more by throwing out one more town I don't want to go to. Why can't he listen? Why can't he get it through his thick head I want to go to Caltanissetta, not *Ir' e Beniri* or even *Iri Sulu?*

"Caltanissetta," I say one more time.

Peppi Rais is not smiling now. Dramatically he gives the rest of the passengers the once-over. He shakes his head the way I've been shaking my head for the past five or six minutes. He rolls his eyes. He clasps his hands, raises them into the air, and pantomimes a desperate man praying to the heavens. Meanwhile the passengers are taking it all in, most of them laughing. Now and then I hear "*Americanu*" as if it were a bad word.

"Caltanissetta," Peppi Rais finally says.

"*Si, Si!*" At this point I am happy again. I have finally made contact. We are communicating. At last he can hear me; the man understands. My hand is in my pocket, I am all ready to ask how much the ticket is when Peppi Rais repeats it again: "Caltanissetta," then adds in his loudest voice so far,

"*Ir' e beniri oppuri iri sulu?*" ["Round trip or one way only?"]

Just as I am about to explode, take little Peppi Rais by the collar of his gray conductor shirt and shake some sense into his empty head, I hear one of the passengers call out in fractured English, "I coulda help you maybe, Mister? 'Splaina to de condotta you wanna Caltanissetta isa fine, bota you go ana return o you joosta go?"

"Roundtrip," I tell him. "Go and return."

The old man smiles, gets Peppi's attention and in Sicilian sets the matter straight. I buy my roundtrip ticket and settle into my uncomfortable seat for the next few hours into Caltanissetta.

On subsequent trips, riding on Peppi's blue bus, he would kid me about those two towns that came right after Serradifalco: *Ir' e Beniri* and *Iri Sulu!*

MICHELI THE FIRST

Born on November 22, 1883, Micheli was the second son of my paternal grandparents Alfonsu Buttaci and Giuvannina Pitonzo. In our family tree he is Micheli the first; my father who was born on July 5, 1905, is Micheli the second, called Michelinu by most of his family.

In most Sicilian families down through the centuries, certain trades and crafts were handed down. Fathers taught sons and sons taught their sons, and in that way they were able to support themselves and their families. The Buttacis were for centuries craftsmen at making shoes, and though they were called shoemakers, they were not what we would call shoemakers today. Back then they did not repair shoes but constructed them according to the actual foot sizes of their customers.

My grandfather Alfonsu had started out as a maker of shoes, but through a bit of good fortune he managed to become a government clerk for the commune of Acquaviva Platani where he and his family lived. Though craftsmen and tradesmen were all respected, only professional people were more highly regarded than government workers. Alfonsu's father Giuvanni, who had fought in Giuseppe Garibaldi's revolution, was also a shoemaker. But the one who showed the most talent and the most promise in this craft of making shoes, was Micheli, Alfonsu's second son. He was also a good singer who, though shy in front of strangers, delighted in singing songs in the company of his many relatives. Micheli was the apple of everyone's eye.

In 1900, when he was only a boy of seventeen, Micheli had on his own invented a shoemaking tool for which other shoemakers, especially his father's brother Zi Luigi, considered Micheli ingenious. My grandfather was so proud of his son that he decided to send him to a trade school for shoemakers, located in the capital city of Palermo, which by car today   from the town of Acquaviva takes about two and half hours. Back then, by horse, who knows how many hours it took!

The tiny Palermo apartment in which Micheli lived while attending trade school was dark and mildewed. His father would later on insist that it was the reason Micheli had fallen ill. Only months after coming to Palermo, he was taken to a hospital and diagnosed with gangrene—more than likely cancer. When the news reached Acquaviva, Alfonsu left immediately to be at his son's bedside.

For the next several months, each weekend Alfonsu would leave his office in the municipal building and make the tiring trip by horse carriage to his son in Palermo. Each visit brought greater sorrow, for he would find Micheli further debilitated, another limb, still another, amputated as doctors tried to arrest the disease. And one could imagine how this father suffered, suspecting that nothing could save his boy. It was only a matter of how much more pain, humiliation, and time remained.

"Papà, please don't come here anymore," Micheli begged him. "To see me like this!"

"*Micheli, figghiu miu.* [Michael, my son,"] said my grandfather to this precious one he loved so dearly, "*sugnu ca pi sentirti cantari.* [I come to hear you sing."] I can imagine Alfonsu—good, sensitive man that he must have been—reach a hand to his son's soft face and caress it gently. The pain my grandfather must have experienced, pain he had to keep hidden inside him in the presence of his dying son! It was a kind of prolonged grief, a mourning before death finally would come and take all of his son from him.

And Micheli would sing still one more song so that during these brief moments of respite neither one of them had to think about the unfairness of someone so young having to die. Micheli, his father would tell the others, never complained. He asked after his mother, his brothers Giuvanni, Paulu, Giuseppi, his sisters Sarafina, Ninetta and Lauretta. He asked about lu Paisi—the town he loved and missed so much. If he was bitter about the hand fate dealt him, he never expressed it to his father on those weekly visits. But it hurt to see the anguish on his father's face each time they'd meet.

"Papà, stay home. I understand. Look how all this brings you so much heartache." But Alfonsu held back the tears. Micheli would lie there in pain but at the same time with much pride for this man who was his loving father.

On September 7, 1902, Micheli died. He was nineteen years old. His father was never the same again. Always a sensitive and reserved man, he became more so with the death of his son. He had what the oldtimers called "*nu cori niccu*, a small heart," which referred to those who lacked the wherewithal to fight even the world if necessary in order to rise above life's misfortunes. Alfonsu was not a fighter. His own father Giuvanni once said, "In this family, not my sons but my daughter Maria Concetta is the real soldier!"

Grief had taken hold of him and would not release him. Grief sang dirges night and day and its voice was Angelic— the voice of Micheli. *"Ti nni cantu sulu un autra, Papà, e poi, pi carità, vatinni a casa. Lassami dormiri!* [I will sing one more, Papa, and then, please go home. Let me sleep!"]

In mid January 1906, at fifty-eight years old, Alfonsu's "small heart" stopped beating. A world cruel enough to take his son away had beaten him. Meanwhile, his last child, my own father, Micheli the second—*Michelinu*—only six months old, lay sleeping in his cradle.

THE LADY IN BLACK

Nowadays, deluged with so many books out there about the supernatural power of angels, as well as with TV programs like *Touched by an Angel* and *Could It Be a Miracle?* few of us would find this story of "The Lady in Black" hard to believe. But not so back in my childhood when my mother first told it to me. It was not only incredible but even frightening. Yet it happened just as I will now recount it.

It was early one summer evening in Acquaviva Platani, the Sicilian village of my parents. The year was 1929. My mother, sixteen years old, sat outside her home on Via Crispi along with her brother Cicciu, 28, their parents Salvatore and Anna Amico, her mother's brother Zi Salvatore Frangiamore, his wife Za Rosaria, their son Toto, 22, Toto's sister and several of his brothers.

Zi Salvatore owned a wine store on the corner across the street, which he had just closed for the night. His son Toto, a well-liked, happy-go-lucky young man sat and enjoyed himself with the family. He had a good reason to be happy: tomorrow he would have a day off from work. Toto worked for a local contracting business where he and another employee would take turns sending sand down a chute to where the other would load the sand onto the delivery truck. It was hard work, but Toto, tall and strong, had served his military duty of two years with the Berseglieri, the toughest infantry unit in the Italian Army. Though he had a slight hearing problem, it had never kept him from hard work or from having a good time.

About 8:00 p.m., while the family sat outside, a young boy came and delivered the message that Toto would have to work the next morning. The news put him off somewhat momentarily, but then needing to get up early, Toto good-naturedly excused himself, said good night, and left for bed.

At ten o'clock the next morning my grandfather and my Uncle Cicciu found themselves at their summer house up on the mountain, a good ten minute walk up Via Crispi. My grandmother—la nonna Anna—stayed at home with my mother. Suddenly beside her in the kitchen appeared out of nowhere an old lady dressed in black like a good number of old Acquaviva women; however, she was not someone Grandma recognized.

Without time to express surprise or to call her daughter, Grandma saw the old woman move behind her, then felt her quickly begin pulling Grandma's long hair in the direction of the door. *"Annuzza, Annuzza, va 'lla portedda!"* [Anna, Anna, go to the entrance of this village!"] the old woman commanded her. But Grandma saw no reason to do that. Her husband and her son were safe up on the mountain in the other direction. Her daughter was somewhere in the house with her. *"Picchì a ghiri alla portedda? Ma figghia ca è. Me maritu e ma figghiu sunnu a muntata nni la casina,"* Grandma explained. ["Why should I go there? My daughter is here. My husband and son are on the mountain in the summer house."]

Three times the lady in black pulled my grandmother's hair towards the door. Three times she insisted she obey her, but three times Grandma adamantly refused. After all, her family was safe. At last the old woman vanished as suddenly as she had appeared.

Grandma was visibly shaken by this visitation, not because the lady in black was of another world. Grandma was accustomed to the paranormal. Most old-time Sicilians are. But she was puzzled as to why the stranger had come.

Less than an hour later neighbors came to her door to tell her that Toto was dead. He had not heard the sand falling down the chute from above where the other worker had released it. As a result Toto had been buried alive. By the time the other worker came down to help him, it was too late.

Perhaps there is a thin line between what may be and what will be. Somehow the old lady in black had tried to intercede, had tried to send my grandmother to the village entrance where Toto was working and call him from his work before it was too late.

SOMEBODY TO TALK TO

The first time I came to Acquaviva Platani I was quite fortunate to not only meet my maternal grandfather Salvatore Amico, but to discover he still remembered the English he learned in the twenty years he lived in New York City back in the early 1900s.

It was October 1965, and Papa To' had been bedridden for the past five years. Back in 1960, while at his summer home up on the mountain, he had ruptured a varicose vein and nearly bled to death. One of the neighbors there saved his life, but he would spend what remained of it lying in bed. Only a year before that his wife Grandma Annina had passed away. He was lonely despite living in the house of his son Cicciu and daughter-in-law Rosalia.

He was an outgoing man who loved talking with people; he was a man everyone considered true to his name: Amico—"friend." So the news of my coming to Acquaviva pleased him very much. He'd have somebody to talk to. It had been eight years since the brief visit of his daughter Giuseppina— my mother—and my sister Anna.

Before that, in 1937, Mama had gone there

with her three children: Alfonsu was five years old;
Giuvanna, who died there, was three; and Anna,
barely one.   As for the rest of us children—Joan,
Sarah, Frank, and I—Grandpa knew us only from
Mama's letters and the photos she mailed him. To
finally meet him was a dream come true!

From October to December 31st when
Grandpa died, I spent as many hours as I could at his
bedside. We hit it off from the start. The first words
he said to me were "Sam, I waited a long time to meet
you!"

And from then on he would tell me stories of
what he remembered of New York City, about the
days when he was the head butler in the Fifth Avenue
home of a very wealthy German-American family
named Dreisden, how he had personally known
Caruso, Henry Ford, King Edward, John D.
Rockefeller, and other notables, including King
Edward of England who years later abdicated the
British throne to marry a divorced woman.

He would tell me stories of when my mother
was a young girl, stories of Acquaviva, stories of the
American soldiers when they came to town during the
liberation of Sicily towards the end of World War II.

After Grandpa died I had no one to talk

English to. It was true I was learning Italian, but still I missed my own language. I would take long walks up and down the steep cobblestone streets and say hello to folks on both sides of the street with a *"Buon giorno!* [Good day!"] and a wave of my hand.

One January afternoon I was walking down Via Giudice when I heard someone call out to me, "Hey, American!" I turned around. "Over here!" called the voice. This time I saw him waving from his front steps where he sat on a wooden chair, one hand in front of him on top of the head of his wooden cane. He was a very old man. I guessed about ninety, but I could've been wrong. Maybe he was 100. He kept waving me forward.

"Buon giorno, Signore," I said.

"Good day," he replied. "What isa you name?"

"Sarbaturi Buttaci. I'm the son of Micheli Buttaci and Giuseppina Amico."

"Where you live?" he asked, motioning me to sit on the other wooden chair beside him. I nodded and sat down.

"America," I said.

"Of course! I know dat. Where in America?"

"New Jersey," I said, and watched him as his

eyes grew large and his almost toothless mouth spread into a smile I at first thought was a yawn.

"Once a befo' I live in Jersey Cit'," said the old man. "I was a shoemake'. I live a dere ten year."

What luck! Not only did I find someone I could sit and talk with, but the man had once lived only a city away from where we once lived in Union City. Excited by my good fortune, I pressed on. "What street in Jersey City? Anywhere near Bergenline Avenue? Did you own your own shoemaker shop?'

The oldest man I had ever seen raised a trembling hand and shook his head. *"Basta! Basta!* [Enough! Enough!"] 'Atsa all I can a speak."

I felt bad. He was old. He needed a rest and I was firing away nonstop questions at him that I realized were too much for him to process all at once. "One question."

Again he raised his hand. *"Basta!* Enough! Atsa all I can a speak. *Ho usatu tutti li palori chi mi rigurdu.* [I used up all the words I remember."] He smiled now, proud that he had recalled so much of that long-ago *lingua brutta*—ugly language—he had struggled with during his time in America. He had recited to me phrases he had managed to save those many years.

Maybe, had we met in Jersey City fifty years before, the old man would have talked a streak We might've learned a lot about each other, but there was not much left to say at this time. Embarrassed, I got up from the chair, nodded my head, smiled, extended my hand—I did everything but speak!

"Facciamu vidiri ogni tantu," he said. ["Let me see you once in awhile."]   I nodded, then stepped down onto the curb and into the street.

"Hey, American," he called out to me.   I turned around.

"Once a befo' I live in Jersey Cit'. I was a shomake'," the old man reminded me.

"You lived there ten years," I said.

"Si! Si! *La Merica!"* he said. *"La Merica!"*

WHATEVER HAPPENED
TO MARIA "THE KNIFE"?

Contrary to misguided opinion, Sicilian nicknames did not originate with mafiosi like "Scarface" Capone, "Lucky" Luciano, Joe "Bananas," and a long list of other gangsters with flashy aliases. Nicknames, or what the Sicilians call *"nnomi nciuria"* or *"suprannomi"* or *"nnumiceddi,"* came about out of necessity. To understand that, we need to talk about the Sicilian custom of assigning birth names.

Though the majority of the island's nearly five million inhabitants live in the major cities of Palermo, Catania, and Messina, the rest reside in hundreds of small villages in the mountains and along the coastal perimeter. These small towners regard city Sicilians with the same wary eye as they do the Italians up north, whom they consider as foreign as any European or American. These villagers still somehow manage to conduct their day-to-day provincial lives some years behind on the time line. The rest of the world is moving too fast for them. The same customs practiced centuries ago are still practiced today, including how the villagers name their newborn.

The first son is named after the baby's paternal grandfather, the second son after the maternal grandfather. The same is true of the first and second daughters: the first is named after the paternal grandmother, the second after the maternal grandmother. All children born after the fourth child are usually named after paternal and maternal uncles and aunts. Add to this the fact that surnames are common in these villages where families are related to one another and usually do not move away. Obviously this doesn't allow for much name variety. Needless to say, the situation can be confusing.

Walking down the streets of Acquaviva Platani, one can hear a mother, a wife, a sister, a friend all calling "Caliddu! Caliddu!" and each of them calling a different Caliddu. It's not unusual that in one family there could easily be ten Caliddu Frangiamores.

I remember when I was a boy, my parents would write letters to Grandpa Salvatore Amico, and under his name on the envelope they'd write *"Fu Francesco,"* ["son of the deceased Francesco Amico,"] my great-grandfather, so the letter would not be delivered to my first cousin Salvatore Amico who lived in the same house. Under Cousin Salvatore's name they'd write *"Di Francesco,"* ["son of the living Francesco Amico,] who was my mother's brother, my Uncle Francesco. Addressing the envelope this way also prevented a letter meant for Grandpa to be opened by Salvatore Amico *fu Antonio* or *di Paolo*, a Salvatore Amico from a different family altogether!

So it makes good sense to attach nicknames to keep the people and the families straight. For example, my mother's first cousin Maria Orlando Siracusa was called Maria "the Knife." Don't ask me how that name came to be. Everyone called her Maria *Cuteddu* so as not to confuse her with another Maria Orlando in town who also had a mother named Giuseppina but was of another Orlando family. No doubt *Cuteddu* was the nickname of Fillippu Siracusa, Maria's husband. This would explain why Maria's brother Giuseppi was not called *Peppi Cuteddu*, but instead *Peppi Gaddu*—Peppi "the Rooster."

Why "rooster"? Who knows! The meaning behind a nickname disappears with time, while the nickname endures from generation to generation.

It was always fun to hear my parents reminisce about *paisani*, villagers, back in Acquaviva. Everybody had a nickname!

There was So-and-So "the Sacristan," who was never a sacristan. He and his family lived near *"la straduna"* [the little street]. "The Sacristan" was the brother of *Chissu* [This-One] or *Chiddu* [That-One], who married Mama's first cousin after her first husband, a second cousin of Papa's, passed away. And then Papa would say, "Do you remember when *Munichiddu* [who was really Monichello] got kicked by his donkey?" Mama would laugh and say, "No, that was Scibetta, the one who was married to the daughter of Sebastianu Vario!" Papa would say, "Not Munichiddu? You're right! It was Scibetta!" because Mama always remembered them all so well, having lived there longer than my father had. And when Aunt Laura was with them, it was a three-way reminiscing with Aunt Laura remembering more than both of them! If either of my parents had a question about someone from Acquaviva, they had only to ask Aunt Laura.

I recall asking my mother once what Grandpa Salvatore Amico's nickname was. My mother smiled. "He didn't have one. The name Amico means 'friend.' That's what he was to everybody!"

As a young girl my mother wanted to try out for a part in a professional theater group that had come to town, but Grandpa forbade her. They would give her a nickname—a stage name—and who would remember Giuseppina Amico?

Years later when I first visited Acquaviva, in 1965, even I got a nickname: *"Lu Spertu,"* ["The clever one."] When the people in Acquaviva tried to make a fool of me, since I didn't know the language that well, I would write their words down, check them later in my huge English-Italian dictionary, and come back the next day with an appropriate response! I felt proud of my new name.

THE NOTEBOOK

Quietly at first, ten-year-old Lauretta Buttaci sat in *Maistru* Germano's classroom, her dark eyes staring down at yesterday's homework composition in her notebook. As usual, the room was silent. *Lu Maistru* [the teacher] did not permit unnecessary distractions in his classroom.

"You are here to learn," he would tell them. "Schoolwork is important business."

The year was 1906. Giuseppi Germano had been Acquaviva Platani's elementary school teacher since the 1870s. He had taught hundreds of children, including Lauretta's sisters Serafina and Ninetta, and four of her brothers, Vanuzzu, the first Micheli, Paulu and Giuseppi. The youngest, the second Micheli, my father, was at the time not quite a year old.

Though he was a stern old man who demanded respect and appropriate classroom behavior, he was also quite patient with his pupils, making it clear that his objective was to instill in them that same love of learning he himself and his wife *La Maistra*, Oliva Pitonzo, both felt.

Signur' Germano stood now at the blackboard, chalk in hand, explaining the day's lesson.

Suddenly he heard her crying, softly at first, as if trying to swallow the sour taste of overwhelming sadness. Almost as one all of the children twisted in their seats to look to the back of the classroom where Lauretta sat now, her face, down on the desk, cupped in her small hands.

Walking slowly to the back of the room, *Lu Maistru* stopped at Lauretta's desk. "Lauretta," he said, a hand gentle on her shoulder. *"Nun chianciri. Lu sacciu cchi si tristi."* ["Don't cry. I know you're sad."] Then she raised her pretty face, framed by long tresses of black hair, and from her seat offered her teacher the notebook. She could not trust herself to speak. He took the notebook from her. Silently he read the composition she had written for homework the day before.

"What does it say?" asked one of the other children.

"Leggilu, Lauretta," ["Read it"] another called.

But Germano raised his hand and the children were quiet again. "This is a very good composition," Germano told her. "I cannot find one mistake in all of it!" When Lauretta lifted her hand for the book, he returned it to her. It surprised him, however, when all at once she stood and began reading her composition to the rest of the class.

First she read the title: "I Miss My Father." Then she paused, cleared her throat, and went on to read the short paragraph she had written. *Lu Maistru* had dismissed them the day before with an assignment to "write something that has special meaning for you." So Lauretta Buttaci now read what she had written. "This year on January 16 my father died. I still have my mother, my sisters, and my brothers, but the house is empty without Papà there. I miss him very much."

Germano brought his hands together and applauded her. With a nod of his head, he encouraged the rest of Lauretta's classmates to do the same. Lauretta closed her notebook.

GRANDPA'S DONKEY IS MISSING

Grandpa Salvatore Amico—*Papá To'*—did not want Grandma's brother Vincinzu Frangiamore to know his donkey was missing. "Tell him," said Grandma. "He'll get the donkey back. If you don't, goodbye donkey!" *Zi* [Uncle] Vincinzu was not an imposing figure in the physical sense: though he was a bit stocky, he was only about 5' 3", and when he spoke, his voice was thin and barely audible. And yet no one dared play him for a fool. He was a tough guy.

He commanded respect from everyone. Even mafiusi—those ruthless gangsters who freely preyed on the frightened—stepped lightly around Zi Vincinzu, who was not in the Mafia. Nor was he a gangster himself, never having taken advantage of anyone for ego or profit. But he made certain he was never dishonored by anyone. He also made sure no one dishonored or hurt in any way members of his family.

"Tell Vincinzu," Grandma said again.

So Papà To' walked the few doors down to his brother-in-law's house where he found him smoking a cigarette on his front steps. "Vincinzu," he called, "Good morning!" Vincinzu saw there was a problem. He could read it in Grandpa's eyes. *"Chi c'è, Sarbatu'? Dimmi.* [What's wrong, Salvatore? Tell me, "] he said.

Visions of an infuriated Vincinzu racing off to find the donkey thief filled Grandpa's head. A man of peace, he'd rather lose a donkey than have the thief harmed in any way. So he hemmed and hawed in an attempt to explain what was wrong.

"Vincinzu, sapiddu si lassava la stadda aperta e lu sceccu nisciu." ["Vincinzu, I wonder if I left the stable open and the donkey walked out."]

Vincinzu laughed. "You? Forget to close the door? Maybe the donkey figured it out and opened the door himself!"

"Cu lu sappi! ["Who knows!"] and Papà To' laughed with him. I had two donkeys; now I have one. What can I say?"

His brother-in-law tapped Grandpa on the shoulder and said, "And you'll have two again, Sarbatu'." He looked at his watch. "Right now it's ten in the morning. By six tonight your missing donkey will find his way back home. *Nun ti scandari."* ["Don't you worry."]

Vincinzu put the word out that Papà To' was missing a donkey, and if whoever was responsible did not return that donkey, he would be missing, too. In a matter of moments Acquaviva Platani was buzzing with the news of the day: Salvatore Amico's donkey was stolen and Don Vincinzu Frangiamore would get it back.

Finally someone in Zi Vincinzu's network of information seekers came back and gave him the culprit's name.

"Cu è? ["Who's there?"] said the voice to Vincinzu's knocking.

"Don Vincinzu Frangiamore."

Immediately the sound of locks and chains as So-and-So hurried to open the door. "Don Vincinzu," said the man, "I'm honored to invite you into my house!"

But Vincinzu did not make an effort to follow him in. "This won't take long," he said. *"Ma cognatu Amico Sarbatu' mi dissi chi nnintra la stadda c'è sulu unu sceccu. C'eranu dui.* ["My brother-in-law Salvatore Amico told me that there's only one donkey in his stable. There had been two.] I've been asking around and someone mentioned your name, that you might be able to help me solve this mystery."

"Whatever I can do, Don Vincinzu," said So-and-So.

"Do you think the donkey opened the gate and walked out?" Vincinzu asked, smiling.

The man tried to return the smile, then settled for shaking his head. "If that donkey doesn't get himself back in the stable by six tonight, I'm in big trouble. I gave my word to my brother-in-law. My word, Signor. *Ci capimu?"* [Do we understand each other?"]

"Whatever I can do, Don Vincinzu," So-and-So repeated.

"E stasira," said Zu Vincinzu, *"quannu viju stu sceccu malandrinu, lu dugnu na pidata nnculu!"* ["And tonight, when I see that naughty donkey, I am going to give him a kick in the ass!"]

The two men laughed; then Don Vincinzu approached So-and-So, reached up on his toes to whisper in his ear. "But if six o'clock comes and goes, somebody's holding that donkey against his will—*Chi pensi tu?* [What do you think?] *Pi sicuru truvarò chistu delinquenti, e faccimuci la cruci!"* [For sure I will find that delinquent, and when I do, we'll make the sign of the cross!]

Zi Vincinzu had made it perfectly clear to the

donkey thief that he had been cut more slack than he deserved. So-and-So now and then nervously eyed his wristwatch. Time was running out. He was anxious for Don Vincinzu to leave so he could be about his business. He had done his business in the middle of the night while Papà To' slept soundly. If he had sold the donkey, he'd have to buy it back while it was still light out without being seen. A small miracle and he knew it. But Don Vincinzu said he'd kick the donkey; what would he do to him?

Grandpa kept indoors as his brother-in-law advised. He worried about the thief. "What's a donkey anyway?" he asked his wife. *"Unu chiù o menu è nenti, Annuzza."* ["One more or less is nothing, dear Anna."]

But Grandma persisted. "Why should we go without what is ours? *Nu latru nni pighhiu pi fissa? Picchì?"* [A thief takes us for fools? Why?"] *Lassalu a Vincinzu."* [Leave it to Vincinzu."]

About 6:15 one of the boys on Via Crispi knocked on Grandpa's door. *"Vossía! Vossía! Zi Sarbaturi! Lu sceccu si tornau! Sava appriri la porta di la stadda!"* [Sir! Sir! Uncle Salvatore! The donkey came back! Open the door of the stable!"] From across the street Vincinzu waved.

SUNDAY HAIRCUTS

Many of my childhood memories center around the kitchen table of all those long-ago Sundays. If I put my mind to it, try getting close to those afternoons, I can mentally conjure up the smell of Mama's spaghetti sauce as she stands there at the stove, stirring away while the rest of us at the table read The *New York Sunday News*. We kids got the funnies.

Earlier that morning Papa, smoking a Lucky Strike outside Most Holy Trinity Church, waited for the nine o'clock mass to let out so he could take us home four or five blocks to 115 Graham Avenue. On the way he'd buy the newspaper and a dozen jelly donuts from the candy and sweets wholesalers on the corner of Graham and Boerum Avenues. In those early years the every-so-often Sunday I dreaded, however, was the one that meant "haircut time" for me. Papa would smile at me and say, *"Ti tagghiu i capiddi."* [I'll cut your hair.] What do you say?" I would go through the usual whining and complaining of a seven- or eight-year-old boy.

"Pa, I don't need a haircut. I just had one.

You always hurt me with the clippers. Next week."
And he'd give me that same old I'm-the-boss-around-
here smile and send me off to fetch a few books to
pile on the wooden chair so I could sit tall enough for
a haircut. Then he'd cover the front of me with part
of an old white sheet and safety-pin it securely behind
my neck. Next he would open the little brown cedar
box containing the two clippers—one of them for
very close work which hurt more than the other one–
–a long, narrow, sharp pair of scissors, a long, black
comb, and without wasting time he'd begin snipping
away.

Oh, the aroma of that cedar box! To this day,
so many years later, if I catch a whiff of cedar wood,
it's as if time gets tricked and I am back to a
Williamsburg Sunday, clearly seeing and hearing my
father again in my memory.

Now and then, while he'd turn to the side to
exchange the manual clippers for the scissors and
comb, I would run my hand over my head to feel how
far he'd gotten.

"Pa, don't cut too much off!" I'd say. And
while he continued cutting, he'd reassure me, "No
worry about it. You got plenty hair. It's summertime.
G.I. haircut looks good. It'll make your hair grow

stronger."

Those haircuts took too long! Papa was a perfectionist, a man who took pride in all that he did, even in those Sunday morning haircuts. It always amazed me years later when I started going to the barber shop how quickly and painlessly they were able to cut my hair. When I told my father about it, his reply was, "Yeah, but I never charged you money, did I?" Years later the barbers small-talked me about baseball, boxing, even politics, but on those torturous Sundays, Papa would cut my hair and talk about my school grades, about the importance of education, about how much he wished he could have gone to college as I would one day go.

He would talk about his growing up without a father, being in the seminary and being expelled from it because he told the truth. "Well, Michael, one day you'll be a priest," said the director priest at the seminary in Caltanissetta, Sicily. "What is it about being a priest that you think you won't like?"

Instead of lying, instead of saying something like "Oh, I'd like everything!" Papa, only fourteen at the time, looked up at that priest and replied, "I don't think I would like very much waking up at all hours of the night to visit the sick and dying." It was the truth as he saw it, but it was enough to send him packing.

The small hairs the scissors snipped away pricked my neck like pins and I would cry out, "Oww! That hurts!" And Papa would say, *"Sta firmu! Nun muovati!"* [Stay still! Don't move!] Then: "You want steps? You think you'd look good then?" By "steps" he meant a layering effect that's so popular today. I shook my head no as slightly as I could without upsetting him more than he already was. *"Comu semu priati,"* he'd go on. ["How wonderful we are!"] A very sarcastic way of saying "You ingrate! "I give up my time to give you a good haircut and instead of thanking me, you complain about a few hairs falling down your neck. Almost finished. A little more."

When he turned away for a change of instruments, I'd again take inventory by touching the top, the sides, and the back of my head. There's nothing there!" I'd say, half crying. "You cut it all off!" Then Papa would send my little sister Joanie for the little mirror so I could look inside and see for myself I was wrong. "See?" Papa would say. "Plenty of hair left. Maybe I should cut a little more." At that point I'd be pulling at the white sheet, feeling back there for the safety pin so I could unhook myself and get down from those tall books before Papa could reach the clippers again.

Meanwhile, dinner was ready. I could smell the *basilicó*, the basil, in the spaghetti sauce and the meatballs. "Go clean up," Papa would say, "so we can all sit down and eat." When I'd get back and we'd all be seated and ready to eat, my mother would say, then my sisters, "What a nice haircut." And I would remember finally to turn to the head of the table where my father sat, and say to him, "Thanks, Pa, for the haircut." He would smile and wink his eye, then he'd look at his good work and nod his head.

ALTAR BOY

If a generalization could be made about the Sicilians I've known in my life, I would say the majority of them have been positive thinkers. Few of them would allow life's setbacks to detain them too long. They recognized problems for what they were; they did not attribute to them more credit or time or concern than they were worth. My father was such a man.

When I was nine years old, back in 1950, the family moved to upstate Utica, New York, from Williamsburg, Brooklyn, where my parents were unable to make a successful go of their Flushing Avenue luncheonette.

In Utica we lived on the first floor while Uncle Joe and Aunt Rosie Palazzolo lived on the second floor of their home at 721 Blandina Street. Aunt Rosie was my mother's first cousin; her mother Giuseppina was Grandpa Salvatore's sister. Aunt Rosie was the sister, by the way, of Maria *Cuteddu* and Peppi *Gaddu*, whom I mentioned to you in an earlier story.

Some blocks away I began attending fourth

grade at St. Agnes School where my teacher, a rather tall, young nun named Sister Joan of Arc, kept all of us towing the line.

One Friday afternoon at dismissal time, as we were stuffing our schoolbags with books and school supplies, Sister Joan of Arc approached me. "Salvatore," she said, "you will be serving at the 9:00 mass this Sunday. Be there promptly at 8:45."

"Me, Sister?" I asked, thinking she meant another student. "Serving mass, Sister?"

Sister smiled. "You, Salvatore. 9:00 mass this Sunday."

I can still remember walking home that afternoon more frightened than I had ever been in my life so far. What did I know about serving mass! It was true that in Sicily, when he was young, my father had studied to be a priest, and that my brother Al was at this time away at a seminary in Sag Harbor, New York, also studying to become a priest. It was true that both of them knew how to serve mass, knew all the proper responses in Latin, knew all the right altar moves. But I had no clue. How was I supposed to learn it all in two days!

That evening my father couldn't help but detect something was wrong. "What's the matter?" he asked me. "You don't look so good. Something wrong maybe in school?"

Without a word I tried to shrug it off, but he wouldn't let me off that easily. "Tell me what happened." So, half sobbing, I tried to get it out what Sister Joan of Arc was expecting me to do.

"So what happens now?" he asked me.

"I don't know, Pa," I said. "I can't serve mass. I don't know how!" And with that I started crying again.

"Wait a minute," he said, then put his arm around my shoulder. "What's the worst thing that could happen?"

"I get on the altar, the priest says something in Latin,and I can't answer him because I don't know the Latin words."

"Then what?" Papa asked.

"I have to make believe I know the words by mumbling something real low so he only hears the other altar boy giving the response."

"Then what?"

"The priest figures it out I don't know the words or he thinks both altar boys are saying the right words."

"Then what?"

Papa sat there patiently listening to me as I tried to envision every mistep of the way. "I trip on the long cassock I have to wear. I drop the book I'm supposed to carry over to the priest. I pour in the wine instead of the water. I spill one of them on top of the altar or on the priest's sleeve." With each reply, Papa would repeat once more, "Then what?" And I would try to find one more dumb thing I would end up doing to make a fool of myself in front of the priest, the other altar boy, and all the people in their pews.

"Then everybody will laugh at me and that'll get the priest really mad," I finally said, not knowing what else to add to the long list of faux pas I'd already rattled off for him.

"Then what?" Papa asked, but when I sat there silently, not knowing what to say to that, he offered his own response. "Let's say the priest, he's really mad now, all right?" I nodded my head. "I mean, he's turning red and blue. He's as mad as anybody could be, all right?" I nodded again. "So here's what he finally does. He walks down from where he's saying the mass towards where you are kneeling next to the bells you forgot to ring at the right time. He reaches out and grabs you by the throat, starts choking you, and nobody comes to pull him off."

"Pa!" I said, trying to interrupt him. "Pa!"

"That priest couldn't take any more of your mistakes so now he's not gonna stop till he kills you."

I was shocked at what Papa was suggesting. I shook my head and said, "That can never happen, Pa."

He ignored me. "The priest ends up killing you. You're laying there dead in front of the whole church. It's hard to believe but you just paid for all your serving-mass mistakes."

I was still shaking my head, still saying, "No, Pa!" when Papa asked, "And then what?"

"And then what?" I repeated, not quite sure what he meant since I was supposed to be lying there dead at the feet of the killer priest.

"You go to heaven, right?" Papa asked. "You gave up your life like a martyr for your religion. You were killed in the line of duty, serving mass, even though you didn't know how. You were killed but you went to heaven. Is that so bad?" Papa asked. "You're in Heaven!"

I was confused. What was Papa talking about? The priest was not about to murder me if I messed up. I would not lose my life no matter how many foolish things I did up there on the altar. I would not be dying for my faith.

"So you see," Papa said, that old familiar philosopher's smile spreading across his face, "the worst that could happen on Sunday would turn out to be the best thing that could happen in your whole life! You have nothing to worry about, Sal. You go there and see I'm right. Don't worry about the Latin. Nobody—not even the Romans!—learned Latin in a day. Everything will be all right. Think positive. Always think positive."

Finally Sunday came. Papa's talk put me at ease. I was scared, but I knew that no matter what happened I'd survive it. As it turned out, I was one of about twenty altar boys at that 9:00 high mass at St. Agnes Church, who would march in procession before and after the mass. We would walk two by two in front of the priest and the two "real" altar boys before the mass began and then later walk two by two behind the priest and the two "real" altar boys when the mass was over. The only Latin I needed to speak was the word "Amen."

My family was there to witness my first "served" mass, and as I walked down the aisle, my father beamed his "wasn't-I-right?" smile at me, and winked his eye the way he always did when he was proud of us. All I could think about was Papa saying to me, "No matter what bad things happen in your life, ask yourself, 'And then what?' and you'll see everything works out for the best."

ANOTHER CUP OF ESPRESSO?

Rare is the Italian or Sicilian home that does not close a good meal, especially on Sundays, with cups of espresso, which we kids growing up called "black coffee." Of course, we were too young to share an espresso with our parents. Papa said it was too strong for kids. Mama insisted it would keep us up all night, which we children thought a good argument for our drinking it on Friday nights when we wanted to stay up and watch the *Late Late Show* on Channel 2. For each of us, drinking that very first cup of espresso became a rite of passage into adulthood.

Years after my first demitasse of espresso, I left America to study in Italy. The year was 1965. The year before, my third at Seton Hall University, I had applied for and was granted a four-year graduate program scholarship at the University of Rome. I applied only after I told my good friend and classmate Ken Diamond, "But I don't speak Italian," and he reassured me with "Don't worry about it. Most Italian universities conduct classes in English for guys like you." He himself spoke Italian rather well; in fact, he planned to attend an Italian university in Perugia.

As it turned out, Ken was wrong about the University of Rome. I lasted there a total of three embarrassing days until my deliverance by a kind professor who took pity on me and accompanied me to the dean, who wordlessly accompanied me to the front door.

Two days after that I was on a train out of Rome on my way to Sicily, where my maternal grandfather Salvatore Amico lived in a small mountain village Acquaviva Platani. In the next few months I managed to learn enough Italian and Sicilian to break my vow of silence and begin to comfortably converse with the villagers.

But let me get back to my espresso story. It was true, as I mentioned, that our parents enjoyed their *tazzi di café niuru* [cups of black coffee] at the end of our meals. My mother would make the coffee in a small imported *cafittera* [coffee pot] that yielded up to four small cups the size of Chinese teacups. When the water climbed bubbling to the top of the spout, Mama would be standing right there to first turn off the gas and then pour a cup for Papa and one for her.

In Sicily I was in for a big surprise! All the

people drank espresso, regardless of their age. And they drank it at different times of the day, not just after dinner. One more thing: the espresso in Acquaviva was thicker, more potent, and doubly more bitter than the Italian-American variety I'd been accustomed to back home.

More popular in Sicily than espresso, however, is respect. It is quite easy to offend people there, without realizing or intending to. My father often told us the story of the two Sicilian families feuding for centuries that finally decides to bury the past, forgive and forget. One of the two families invites the other for an elaborate Sunday dinner, which the other family attends. All is going well. Neither family mentions the feud or how many cousins and uncles and brothers were murdered as a result of it or how the feud began or who was right or the slightest word that would upset this peaceful assembly. But at the end, after a sumptuous dinner with countless courses, the host offers the head of the other family a final cup of espresso to help digest all this good food, but the man declines. He's too full, he tells him. He just can't, he says. The host takes this as an affront to his wife, who has worked so hard to cook the meal, to brew the coffee, to serve those who only days before had been sworn enemies. What happens next? The feud is back in full force!

So I was very conscious of doing nothing to offend these people. It was bad enough I was from America, which most of the villagers considered Sin Country, but I was also the son of Micheli Buttaci and Giuseppina Amico, both from here, both with the same values these people believed in, both having doubtless passed on these values to their children. I was therefore on my best behavior.

With little to do in a small town that had almost nothing by way of entertainment, everyday I'd walk up and down the different cobblestone streets and wave hello to the people who stood in doorways or sat on their stone steps. *"Buon' giorno! Buon' giorno!"* ["Good day! Good day!"] I would greet them. And almost everyone of them would reply, *"Si trasi."* ["Come in."] And not to offend, I would enter their homes, sit and talk with them at table, until always the woman of the house would ask me, *"Sarbaturi, ti pigghi café oppuri Amaru Sicilianu?"* ["Salvatore, will you take espresso or Amaro Siciliano?"]

I had tasted Amaro Siciliano but found it much too bitter; besides, it made me a little tipsy if I drank too much of it. At least the bitterness of the coffee could be corrected with several lumps of sugar. *"Mi pigghiu café, grazie, Signura."* ["I'll take coffee; thanks, Maam."] After drinking the coffee, I'd explain I had to finish my walk or go visit my cousin Alfonsina or Isabella or Padre Alfonso or Aunt Serafina, who was waiting for me; and with that I'd be gone.

I've described the potency of the Sicilian espresso. Did I mention how in America one demitasse of Medaglio D'Oro espresso once a week was about all I drank? Have I told you yet one of my father's favorite maxims? "Do everything in moderation. Too much of anything is no good."

On a typical day in my first two weeks in Acquaviva, I would visit at least ten or eleven homes, and at each of them I would decline the Amaro Siciliano and accept a cup of espresso. Maybe two cups. That's at least ten or eleven cups of espresso a day, which did not include the ones I had at breakfast, at lunch, at dinner, and often one before going to bed.

It was inevitable that it would all catch up with me. It happened finally one night as I lay in bed on the second floor of Zi Cicciu and Za Rosalia's house. I slept in the bedroom next to theirs. It was a huge living room that my uncle and aunt had converted into a bedroom for me. Instead of a couch, they had gotten me a bed to sleep in and they had brought in a bureau for my clothes. It was in that room I woke up in the middle of a terrible nightmare in which thousands of bugs were racing all over my body! I would try to pull them free of my skin but they held on tenaciously, burrowing themselves deeply beneath the hot surface of my skin.

I forced myself awake. Except for the bugs, it was no dream. My skin was hot and crawling; I was itching all over and it was painful. It felt as though under my skin those nightmarish bugs were trapped and trying to liberate themselves by boring through my flesh.

I got up from the bed and walked to Zi Cicciu and Za Rosalia's bedroom door. I knocked a couple of times and when my uncle asked what was wrong, I could not speak! I felt the words in my throat but I couldn't push them out. Frightened, I began rapping loudly on the door. When my uncle opened it, he took one look at me, and turned to his wife. "Send Fontana's boy to get Dr. Milano!" he ordered. Then he took my arm and led me back to the bed. The look on his face said I was in a lot of trouble. The way I felt, I already knew that.

At last Dr. Milano was standing at the side of the bed, looking down at me. His black leather bag he placed beside me. "What's wrong?" he asked me. I found my voice again and said, "I don't know. My skin is killing me," and with that I started scratching my arms till they bled a little.

"Drinking a lot of coffee?" the doctor asked.

"Yes, Doctor."

"Five cups? Six? Ten?" he wanted to know.

"Almost twenty," I said. Dr. Milano shook his head as if to say These Americans! They're not too smart!

"You could've killed yourself. That much coffee could boil your blood. A few more days and you would be dead. Where's the blood going to go if it gets too hot like that?" he wanted to know. I shrugged. "Burst through the veins, that's where!" he said. He gave me something. Maybe a shot. Maybe pills. Who remembers now. "From now on, they offer you coffee, you tell him Dr. Milano won't let me accept. No more coffee, you hear? You come here to visit your grandfather and you end up nearly dying before that old man!"

After that I did what the good doctor ordered. I politely said no. Now and then I took a little shot glass of Amaro Siciliano but never more than one a day. I had learned my lesson: "All things in moderation. Too much of anything—even friendly little cups of espresso—can be a bad thing."

HOW WILL I KNOW TRUE LOVE?

The first girl who ever turned my head was Helen Steubel, back when I was in grade school at St. Benedict Labre's in Richmond Hill, New York. There had been other girls before Helen, but none who could start my heart racing and the palms of my hands perspiring as Helen could. Though we were both sixth graders, we shared no classes, both of us assigned different home rooms. The times I did see her—in the school corridor, on the playground, at dismissal when she'd be walking in the opposite direction towards home, my reaction remained constant: I would stand there immobilized, my eyes unblinking in a kind of catatonic stare broken only by the ribbings I'd get from the boys in my class. I was smitten; of that I had no doubt. Paris had his Helen of Troy. I had my Helen of Richmond Hill. Her initials I doodled in all my notebooks. Drawing hearts of all sizes came easily, my initials above, her initials below that capital "L" that I'd spear with cupidian arrows!

"What's the matter with you?" my father

asked me one night after dinner as I sat at the kitchen table, daydreaming through my homework. "You all right? You walk around like a guy in a fog. You sick?" I moved one of the two piles of schoolbooks out of his way. He sat down beside me. "An hour already," he went on, "and the books—what are you waiting for? The books ain't gonna read themselves to you. You gotta open 'em and read 'em."

"Pa," I began, "I think I'm in love." It caught him off guard because he went big-eyed and pursed his mouth the way he did whenever he was deep in thought or heard something that needed to be mulled over.

"In love?" he asked. "A boy eleven and in love. Hmmm," he said, nodding his head. "Love."

"I think so, but I'm not sure it's really love, or just, you know, just——"

"Infatuation," he offered. I nodded, figuring that must be what it is when it's not really love. "You're not sure so far," my father said, like some attorney reviewing a case.

"Maybe it's love; maybe it's not love."

"Pa, she's beautiful! She's got long red hair, freckles on her face, blue eyes—"

"Irish," he said.

"German, Pa. Her name is Steubel. Helen Steubel. She's in a few of my classes. I think I'm falling in love with her, Pa!"

"And she loves you, too?"

"That I don't know. It's hard to tell."

"You mean this is one-way love?" he wanted to know. "You're falling in love and she's not falling. What do you mean? What does she say?"

I turned my eyes away, stared absently down at my social studies book, which I had been opening and closing in my nervousness. Papa put his hand down on the open book. "I haven't talked to her yet."

Papa laughed. "Okay, one-way love. Now what?" Just then Mama walked into the kitchen and he winked his eye at her the way he'd do when something good was coming, something he was going to say that was worth remembering. I pretended I didn't notice. "You want to know if this Helen business is love, right?" I nodded.

"You think love happens like this?" he asked, snapping his fingers. I shrugged my shoulders. "That fast?"

Now I knew I had him. How could he argue this one. "Pa, you and Mama fell in love at first sight.

She was coming from the bakery, carrying a loaf of bread down the street on her way home. You were coming up the street with a friend of yours when you saw her. When she saw you. And you both fell in love! Isn't that how it happened?"

"Wait a minute now," he said.

"No, Pa. What happened to you and Mama could happen to me and Helen Steubel once I get her to look at me and stop for a minute and talk a little." Now he and Mama were both smiling.

"Love at first—"

Papa suddenly took on his serious face. Raising his hand, he stopped me in mid-sentence. "Now wait a minute," he said again. You want love or you want true love? Come on."

"True love," I replied. Who in his right mind would choose love over true love. "True love, of course, Pa."

"Your mother and I, we love each other, maybe from that first minute I saw her on the road home that night. Who knows? And since then we keep loving each other everyday, more and more. I love her; she loves me. I'd cut off my right arm for your mother. You know why? Because that woman would cut off her right arm and her left for me! So we love each other, all right? But is it true love?" I waited for him to continue, but he wanted an answer. "Is it?"

"Sure it's true love. What else?" I said. "You and Mama have true love."

Now he was shaking his head, looking pensive again, narrowing his eyes as he said, "I don't know that for sure. She don't know that either." Now I was big-eyed. My parents did not have true love? If *they* didn't, who did?

"Let me tell you what true love is, Sal," he began. "It's not so easy. Love? Love is easy. Everybody loves everybody. Kisses and a box of candy, some flowers, Honey here, Honey there. Oh, yeah, love is very easy. But does it last? Does everybody stay in love? Some of them do, but not all of them."

"Pa," I started, but he was not going to be interrupted.

"Here's where true love comes in. Your mother and I, we love each other every single day. We live this way like we have true love. This is what we want to believe. But do we have true love?"

"You don't?" I asked.

"We have love and we are praying we have

true love, but when do we find out for sure? When do you find out Helen is your true love? Or Mary? Or whoever you fall in love with, who falls in love with you? When do you know true love when it comes? Now here's the hard part, so listen to me. You don't know what you had all along was true love until one of you is on the deathbed and the other one is still there taking care of the other one, making dying easier, not just there because he or she has no place else to be or stayed all those years out of habit or duty. I mean still there and truly in love. That's when you can look back and say, 'We had true love! We were not just in love; we were truly in love!"

"But Pa, you have to wait until you're almost dead or the one you're married to 's almost dead to find out what you had all along? True love?" I could not believe what I was hearing. Everybody everywhere was waiting on line to fall in love, and here was my father telling me love was easy. True love was another matter. To me, an eleven-year-old boy who had, and did not have, Helen Steubel, true love seemed desirable but probably unattainable in my lifetime.

Then Papa affectionately put his arm around my shoulder as we sat beside each other at the kitchen

table.   "Someday when you meet that woman—
wherever and whoever she is—live everyday showing
this true love to each other. Tell yourselves you two
are the lucky ones and someday you'll find out for
sure it was true love. Someday at the end of all those
days together you'll know for sure then." He glanced
up at the kitchen wall clock.

"Hey! You better do your homework. It's
getting late. What do you think Helen is doing right
now, huh? She's doing her homework!" We laughed.

Many years later when Papa was on his
deathbed, and Mama was there for him all those
agonizingly sad and depressingly fleeting days, I
remembered that kitchen-table talk of his. There was
Papa, always so strong and positive, lying there in his
final time, but not alone. There was Mama, always
there for him, loving him even beyond their long
married lives, loving him all these days since he's been
gone.

On one of those last hospital visits, perhaps a
week before Papa passed away in his St. Mary's
hospital bed, on a respirator, he lay there unable to
speak. I tried to read the expression on his face, the
message in those once sparkling eyes that now
drooped with drowsiness and flinched with pain.

Once he smiled at me, nodded toward Mama, nearly managed to wink at me.

I know, Pa, what you were trying to tell me that April evening. I hadn't forgotten that childhood talk, your wisdom repeated now without the sound of words: "Look at this woman sitting beside me," those eyes seemed to say. "She's still with me, still my true love, after all these years."

A CASTLE, THREE SISTERS, AND A BARON

It was a long time ago in the late 1300s, in the environs of feudal Manfreda, an ancient hamlet from which present-day Mussomeli, Sicily, would arise. Baron Manfredi Chiaramonte was the master of all Manfreda, and he constructed a castle high as an eagle's nest atop a rocky abutment. This castle was always locked shut; rarely did its doors open and then only to those the baron held in absolute trust.

With him in the castle lived his wife, a young and very beautiful woman. Along with them lived her two older, unmarried sisters, who dearly loved the baroness, and distanced themselves from castle matters, preferring instead to spend most of their time praying in the chapel.

One day King Frederick IV dispatched an order to all his barons, including Chiaramonte, to assemble and equip their soldiers with weapons, horses, and necessities, and lead them to Palermo to assist the king in his war against his enemies.

When he read the communique, he was ecstatic. After all, he was well prepared for the field of battle where he had already proven himself quite honorable.

The only displeasure he experienced was the thought of leaving alone in the castle his lovely wife of whom he was insanely jealous. Should he resort to torturous instruments to prevent infidelity as did other nobles? No, he could not be that cruel.

Gathering his wife and two sisters-in-law in the grand salon, he revealed to them the contents of the king's demand upon which he needed to act immediately. It meant he was leaving the castle.

First, however, he would have to attend to their security. He explained that they'd be safe within the castle. He would provide them with enough food for two months: more than a generous amount of time since he reassured them the war would end weeks before then. In addition, under a back terrace there was a spacious room he assigned them, which he intended to wall up! Inside that room he would leave them four narrow loopholes—small elongated portholes—for air and sunlight and a place from which to throw refuse.

This done, assured of the abundance of provisions, Baron Chiaramonte proceeded to wall up the room's only door with limestone, embrace at length all three of those poor creatures, and then gallop on his thoroughbred towards Palermo.

The military rally took place at the piazza in Kalsa, once the place where the Saracene emirs held court and now the parade grounds for Sicilian feudal lords to demonstrate the splendor of their armor and the precious harnesses of their horses. Lances, swords, daggers sparkled in the sun. Horses pawed as if fuming to pitch themselves into the winds of war. Meanwhile, the foot soldiers, already fed, were grooming their masters' mounted horses. There they were: an ostentatious display, an unbroken parade line of barons and knights astride horses, and straight-backed soldiers on foot. They were on their way to Palermo where they would entreat the king's blessing as they marched off to war.

Meanwhile, back at the castle, during the first days of seclusion, the three sisters locked in that room, were not only not suffering there, but they were enjoying the novelty of the situation. It elevated their spirits. They talked endlessly, laughed, and worked: the days passed slowly, but they managed to fill them with activity which earned them a deserved night's sleep.

After two weeks the days became somewhat wearisome. The baroness had grown plump, perhaps because her older sisters, in order to save her any exertion, kindly excused her from any labor, and this inactivity showed on her.

After the first week of the first month, the sisters hastened to draw up an inventory of available provisions so they could ration them among themselves. They sought to get by with the least possible share of food because they knew if they ran out, being secretly walled up as they were, since no one knew about their confinement, no one could help them.

It was this strict rationing that brought them to see in one another how each was losing weight, but none dared express it for fear it would add to the dread and discomfort of growing so thin.

When a month had passed, the sisters thought only of the return of the baron. They busied themselves calculating how much longer; they counted the days, discussed the fortunes of war he'd bring back, fancied even the date of his probable return. They hoped his return would be soon.

Meanwhile, the days passed and despite the limitations courageously met, the three sisters watched the level of the flour sack go down. The oil in the jar was now only a few fingers high, and therefore, limited the use of the lamp. The biscuits were nearly gone. The water in the containers was diminishing.

Two months went by very slowly, like a sad, painful dripping. In their hearts they lacked a place now for hope. This ordeal tragically marked them. They'd look at one another and discover new furrows lining their foreheads. They saw their faces haggard and thin, eyes sinisterly anticipating empty-eyed skulls. They shuddered in these thoughts, but then they comforted one other with religious talk, giving their hearts to the greater faith—Divine Providence.

By now the supplies were nearly exhausted, and the noble Chiaramonte had not yet returned. Had he died in battle? they wondered. But his death, they knew, would be a sentence of death for the three of them. To survive a day longer, they decided to alternately eat one day and fast the next. Their main objective was to stay alive. But even so, some mouthfuls of food were necessary: a remedy against dying.

As we said, the supplies were almost gone. It was clear that if the baron did not arrive in time, all three sisters would die of hunger. Already the oldest could no longer stand; she was frighteningly debilitated. The middle sister complained of continuous headaches. Only the youngest, the baroness, still maintained her strength, but she cried incessantly that her Manfredi had died in battle.

Every so often, especially in the morning when the farmers were known to crowd the countryside, the baroness would approach one of the loopholes and scream as loudly as she could, "Help! Help!"

But all four loopholes faced the back entrance of the castle where no one passed. The room had become a prison cell. It was too high in the castle; no one would hear her screams.

In the almanac next to the lamp of one of the loopholes, one of them had marked the days of their captivity: Day 92. After three months, all the food was gone. Even the water in the huge jars standing on the marble floor were standing on their last legs. Now and then a sense of desperation took hold of them, except for the oldest, who was resigned to dying, no longer spoke nor complained. Only her lips moved now and then in a mumbled prayer to Our Lady of Chains.

The middle sister, instead, forced herself to argue in favor of keeping the faith that they'd survive.

But hunger gnawed at the gut, and there was nothing left to eat. The middle sister remembered that her book of daily devotions was bound in parchment made with animal skin, and therefore edible. She detached the book cover, cleaned it, and cut it into tiny pieces. Then, like a priest to his communicants, she placed a small piece in the mouth of the baroness. It was difficult chewing and swallowing that material, but it was imperative she do so. The image of her husband returning from war impelled her to chew heartily, moving her head like a poor dog, each time she moved her jaw.

"Now you two eat," said the baroness to her sisters, when she realized perhaps this little shred she had swallowed might allow her one more tomorrow. However, when she fed a piece to her oldest sister, the woman tightened her lips in a sign of revulsion. She could no longer speak.

"You take it," the baroness said to the middle sister.

But she took only a very tiny sliver and the rest she saved in a towel like some sacred relic. "It's important that you survive," the middle sister said. "For us, life at this point is ending."

Warm tears filled the eyes of the baroness as

she stood in that gloomy corner of the castle which had gradually become for them an exile, a prison, and soon enough a tomb.

Time passed unyieldingly. Now the water was gone. To the screams for help launched by the baroness from the narrow loophole, only murders of crows responded with funereal songs.

At last the oldest sister had died, composed in her bed with a small holy picture still pressed at her lips. The middle sister prepared to follow her into a sky never before this so dearly longed for. The youngest sister vacillated between bouts of black sadness and of techno-colored moments of optimism.

One night she fell asleep and dreamed her Manfredi had returned to liberate her from this horrific torment, but when she awoke in the dimness of morning twilight, she saw even her middle sister's eyes wide open to death's kind enlightenment. She shook her but her sister remained still. She held the lifeless hand against her breaking heart. She had died of starvation perhaps only several hours before.

Now she alone remained to suffer the acute thirst that could not be quenched, for the water jugs were dry as dust. Approaching the loophole to cool her throat, without satisfaction she inhaled the sultriness of summer. She tried to cry for help, but to her meager voice only the swallows made warbling replies.

***

At his sumptuous royal palace, decorated in Norman splendor, King Frederick IV received the returning baron, and when they came face to face, the king embraced him with words of salutation and praise.

"We know you have comported yourself as befitting a hero, but fortune has not served you well. Willingly we have procured your ransom and we are pleased to welcome you home. Here in our court you may remain as long as you desire."

"Master!" replied Manfredi Chiaramonte, "Your benevolence is the truest reward I could ask for, and I am profoundly indebted to you. But I ask your grace to permit me to leave Palermo immediately, for my wife awaits me in her walled castle room."

"Walled?" asked the astonished king. "Then race quickly and restore her to the air and light. Take with you the good wishes of your king."

"Master! My wife will be so elated to receive your kindness as I too am content. I thank you once more for paying the ransom that freed me. I will remember your deed all the days of my life, and this same life of mine will always be at your disposal."

Leaving the palace, procuring a good horse, the baron left for his castle in Manfreda. In a gallop, in a trot, in a gait, all according to the nature of the terrain.

He followed the course of the river, sparse of water, then ascended for Michenese for the hills as far as the plateau from where he could see his castle, jutting high on a cliff of reddish stone and green thickets. His heart beat furiously. His dear angel awaited him there in that castle. Quickly he ordered some workers with pickaxes and hammers to take down the walled door, all the while repeating in his loudest, most forceful voice the sweet name of his wife. But no one answered.

When the stones fell away, the room appeared like a huge dark tomb. In one corner, in their beds, the two sisters-in-law lay decomposing. On the floor, under one of the loopholes, lay his wife, her flesh still radiating a washed-out rosiness, for she had been dead only a short time.

Eyes brimming and overflowing with tears, the baron nonetheless stared at this horrible place, then screamed the name of his dead wife over and over again like a litany to the dead. From the narrow loopholes he could hear the hoarse cry of crows staccatoing the soft chirping of the summer swallows.

Translated by the author from an Italian book written by his late cousin whose family originally came from Mussomeli, the city of the castle, before later settling in nearby Acquaviva Platani.

Father Alfonso Giannino, S.J. "Un Castello, Tre Sorelle, e un Cavaliere" from: LA FIERA DEI RICORDI: CORTOMETRAGGI SU MUSSOMELI E MUSSOMELESI. ["A Castle, Three Sisters, and a Baron" from: THE FAIR OF MEMORIES: SHORT DOCUMENTARIES ABOUT MUSSOMELI AND ITS INHABITANTS.] Caltanissetta, Sicily: Edizioni Lussografica, 1990; pages 189-194.

POEMS

*"What will become of us when the names
behind the pictures smudge with age?"*

from: "These Words"

MAMA'S ANGEL PRAYER

"I sleep with four angels:
two at my head,
two at my feet,
and the little Baby Jesus
in the middle of us all!"

This is what my mother learned in Sicilian
when she was a girl in Acquaviva Platani.

*"Iu mi curcu cu quattru ancili,
dui susu, dui iusu,
e Gesuzzu nni menzu."*

It kept the demons out of her bed;
it helped her fall asleep in her dark room.

Today after ninety-four years of light and dark,
still she says the prayer of her four guardian angels,
still she keeps the candle of her faith flaming brightly.

WEEPING FOR SICILY

For the land that is barren,
the trees without olives,
Vineyards unyielding,
We weep, we weep.
For your children all leaving
On trains to big cities,
Mothers and fathers,
We weep, we weep.

For the hot sun upon us,
The rain hardly falling,
Mountains on fire,
The poor and the tired,
The old who are lonely,
The piazza now empty
We weep, we weep.

For those moments unfriendly,
Long days slowly crawling,
Swift years that wear wings,
Old songs we stopped singing,
Dark eyes filled with longing,
A laughter grown quiet;
We weep, we weep

CHIANTU PI LA SICILIA

Pi lu tirrenu nun cultivatu,
Olivitu senz'olivi,
Vigniti senza racina,
Chiancemu, chiancemu.

Pi toi figghi chi partianu
Su treni a citá granni,
Matri e patri,
Chiancemu, chiancemu.

Pi lu suli caudu supra nuautri,
La pioggia pocu cadi,
Li muntagni bruciati,

Li puuri e li fatigati,
Li anziani abbannunati,
La chiazza vacanti,
Chiancemu, chiancemu.

Pi ddi momenti ostili,
Iorna lunghi strisciannu,
Li anni veloci chi indussanu li ali,
Pi li canzuni antichi nun cantamu chiú,
Occhi scuri chini di la vogghia,

For what life has denied us,
For the graveyard inside us,
For houses all empty
Of your daughters and sons.

Somewhere in London
Go letters unanswered.
We weep, we weep

For promises broken,
High hopes left unopened,
These tears that are choking,
we weep for you, Sicily,
Oh, we weep.
We weep.

Pi chidda ca la vita nni rifiutau,
Pi lu cimiteriu dintra nuautri,
Pi li casi vacanti di vustri figghi.

In quarchi parti di Londra
Littri vannu senza risposta.
Chiancemu, chiancemu.

Pi prumissi rumbuti,
Pi spiranzi abbannunati,
Sti lagrimi chi nn'affucanu,
Chiancemu pi tia, O Sicilia,
Chiancemu, chiancemu.

SICILIAN GRANDMOTHER

Nonna you said bent over in neighborhood fields
picked dandelion spring times
arthritic fingers squeezed bloodless
through tight scissor rings
   Snipping, snipping.

Nonna you said passed winters craving dandelion
salad greens, dreamed of salad bowls
filled to overflowing with her delicacy
that she valued more than the gold
sought after by the conquistador Pizarro.
Nonna, waiting anxiously for each spring,
accepted the challenge of the harvest with joy:
It was her liberation.

Nonna you said fed all of you,
filled salad bowls of danelionmania:
   "Eat! Eat!"
How you all wished Sicilian nonna would convert,
sacrifice at the lettuce counter
like those American grandmothers,
but she would nod her head,
biding time, dreaming of next spring.
Now you say the family misses her green gifts,
that you all mourn the manna of dandelion
that no longer roars from the heavens.

NONNA SICILIANA

Mi diceste che chinava per raccogliere il dente-di-leone
ogni primavera in aperta campagna vicina.
Le sue diti artritice e esangui
la nonna si strizzava negli
anelli dei forbici e ne tagliava, tagliava...

La nonna, mi diceste, ogn'inverno sentiva
troppo la mancanza del dente-di-leone,
anche sognava spesso d'un' insalatiera pieno
di questo cibo ghiotto che ella valutava
di più dell'oro che i conquistatori cercavano.
La nonna con ansia aspettava la primavera,
accettava con gioia la sfida della raccolta:
la sua liberazione.

Mi diceste che nutriva a voi tutti,
riempiva l'insalatiera trabocca del dente-di-leone:
"Mangiatelo! Mangiatelo!"
Come voi speraste un giorno la nonna siciliana
si covertirebbe, preferirebbe la lattuga
come le nonne americane, ma ella con un cenno di sì,
pensava la prossima primavera.
Ora mi dite che voi, la sua famiglia,
sentite la mancanza dei suoi regali verdi,
e vi dolete per la manna del dente-di-leone
che mai più ruggirà dal santo cielo.

MY HANDSOME FATHER

Where is my handsome father?
Have you seen him?
Tell me where he is.

With his sister Serafina or with his sister Lauretta
or with Ninetta? With his brother Vanuzzu
or with his brother Paulu or with Giuseppi?
With his father whom he'd never seen?
With his mother (oh, what joy!)
With his daughter Jenny,
his angel with the soft, blond hair?
With his son Frank? His daughter Anna?

Where is my good father?
Nearby somewhere in this same world
or far away, farther than the moon?
The same tears which he shed
we now continue to weep.
One moment he was here:
His face sad and pained, a mask of suffering.
The next moment his body finally slept
and found that holy place upstairs,
while we, like miserable orphans,
search in vain now for his smile.

My brave father-- Where is he?
Have you seen him?

ME PATRI BEDDU

Me patri beddu, unni è?   L'aviti vistu?
Pirchì nun mi nni diciti nenti?
Unn'è me patri?
Cu la pipina Serafina o cu la soru Lauretta,
o cu la soru Ninetta?
Cu lu pipinu Vanuzzu o cu lu frati Paulu,
opuru cu Giuseppi?

Cu so patri chi mai lu a'vistu?
Cu so matri (O, chi gioia!) Cu la figghia Gioannina
so ancilu cu li capiddi biunni e lisci?
Cu so figghiu Franciscu? Cu la figghia Anna?

Me patri bonu, unni è?
Vicinu nni chissu stissu munnu o luntanu,
chiu luntanu di la luna?
Le stisse lagrimi chi iddu chiancì
nuautri cuntinuamu chianciri ora.
Un momentu fu cca; avia la facci trista, dulurusa,
una mascara di sofferenza. Poi lu corpu addurmisciutu
finalmenti trovau la santa paci susu,
mentri nuautri iusu (comu li mischini orfani)
cerchiamu in vanu ppi un so sorrisu.

Me patri bravu, unnu è? L'aviti vistu?
Pirchì nun me nni diciti nenti?

With the saints to whom he prayed?
 Walking beside Our Lady of the Light?
With the angels whom he loved:
Raphael, Gabriel, and Michael?
The gentleman that he always was
still acts as he did here, greeting everyone he meets:
"Let's shake hands.
Day and night no longer exist here.
 So it's Good Eternity to you! Good Paradise!"

Where is my dearest father?
Have you seen him?
Tell me where he is.

People say "He died and that is that!"
People say "You'll find him in the air, a part of all
unseen."
People say "He lives! He lives forever; his pain is
gone."
Have you seen my father?
I need to be certain that his mouth,
in his final days so silent, now smiles and speaks
again,
now prays for all of us and says he will love us
forever.
Who could've believed we'd have reached so sad a
day!
This emptiness can never be filled till I see him again.
For the meantime my courage is a fragile thing.

When I was a child crying, filled with uncertainty,
my father dispelled that fear with sweet, soothing
words.
I believed he'd always be there because he was
honorable,
a man who kept his promises.
No one else anywhere was ever like him!

Where is he?

Unn'è me patri? Cu li santi a chi pregava?
camminanu accantu la Madonna di la Luce?
Cu li ancili chi amava: Rafaelu, Gabrielu, e Michele?
Gentilomi chi iddu era ancora aggisci comu prima,
salutannu tutti quanti, comu gia facivi:
"Stringiamu li mani! iurna, notti-- cca nun cci sunnu cchiù.
Allura, Bon' Eternitaà e Bon Paradisu!"

Unn'è me patri?
Li genti dicunu a mia: "Murì e nun cc'è cchiù."
Qualcun'autru dici: "Lu truvi nell'aria
  facinnu parti di chiddu chi nun si vidi."
Poi n'autru ancora dici a mia:
"Vivi! Iddu vivi ancora e nun suffri cchiù!"
L'aviti vistu me patri beddu? Vugliu essiri sicuru
chi so vucca allultimu silenziusa
ora sorridi e parla e prega pi nuautri
e ci amerà pi sempri! Cu lu putìa mai cridiri ca a sti iorna
avimmu arrivari! Stu votu nun sarà incutu finchì lu vidi;
pero pi ora me corraggiu e nicareddu.
Me patri bonu, unni è? L'aviti vistu?
Pirchì nun nni diciti nenti?

Na voti quannu fu un picciriddu,
chinu di l'incertizza e chiancivu,
me patri cu parole duci disperdiva me paura.
Iu cridivu chi sempri si faceva vidiri
pirchì iddu fu un galantomu di parola
(di tutti banni nuddu c'eranu comu iddu): Unnè e?

Have you seen him? My handsome father?
If I listen now to the wind, I hear his voice,
I hear him speaking to his favorite sister:
"Lauretta, that one over there on the left;
isn't he Mamma's brother Uncle Baldassari?"

Where is my father, man of honor and virtue?
He is living eternity with his family.
In due time we will all reunite:
Mamma, my brothers, sisters, relatives.
Papa in heaven, we will never forget you!
True love never ends; We will find you in Paradise.
Handsome father, all of us happy together,
Once more I will make you weep with laughter!

Ppi cumminazioni, si iu ascutu a lu ventu,
sentu la so vuci chi parla cu la soru favurita,
"Lauretta, chissu dda a sinistra
nun è lu frati di la Mamma? Zi Baldassari?"

Me patri, omu d'onuri e virtu vivrà la vita eterna
cu so famigghia
e pocu passa cu nuautri videmma: mia Mamma, mei frati,
mei sori, mei parinti.
Papà 'n celu, nun ci scurdiamu a tia!
Lu veru amuri nun si finiscia mai
e ti vennimu a truvari in Paradisu!
Papa beddu, cu tia nsemmula e filici
arreri ridimu, arreri ti fazzu chianciri di risata!

THESE WORDS

What will become of us
When these words are gone?
These beats from Sicilian hearts forever stilled?
These words that link us to our beginnings?

What will we finally do when these words are gone?
When time has robbed the gems
From the jewelry boxes of our numbered days?
These words that sing us hymns of salvation?
What will become of us when the names
behind the pictures smudge with age?
Pictures of Mamma, Papa, this uncle, that aunt,
Grandma, Grandpa, the cousins--

Sepia faces brightened by time
Fade like their names
Then slip deep inside us
And even after we give up our breaths,
We will never surrender these words

these words
Sewn in the hem of our souls
These Sicilian words that lightened our hearts
These words
Our departed so freely and so lovingly
Once gave away.

STI PALORI

Chi nni succedirá
Quannu sti palori scumpariannu?
Sti palpiti di cori Siciliani pi sempri cueti?
Sti palori chi nni connettinu a li nustri origini?

C'ama fari finalmenti
Quannu sti palori scumpariannu?
Quannu li anni arrubbarannu li gemmi
Di la cascitedda di li iorna cuntati?
Sti palori chi nni cantanu inni di sarvazioni?
Chi nni succedirá
Quannu li nnomi darreri li ritratti
Si mbrattarannu cu tempu?
Ritratti di Mama, Papá, stu ziu, dda zia,
La nonna, lu nonnu, li cugini--

Facci (niuru di siccia) troppu illuminati du suli
Sculurannu comu li soi nnomi
E poi s'affunnannu nnintra di nuautri.
Anchi doppu chi pigghiaremu l'ultimu respiru,
Mai e poi mai tradiremu sti palori

Sti palori cusuti ni l'orlu di l'armi.
Sti palori Siciliani chi sullivanu li cori
Sti palori chi nu passatu li morti nustri nni rigalaru
Accussí vulinteri cu tantu tantu amuri.

A WALK IN THE PIAZZA

While we Acquaviva townspeople
sleep the quiet night away,
there in the Piazza Plado-Mosca
an incredible crowd gathers
as though it were afternoon!

High above the cobblestone street,
without touching ground, they walk arm in arm,
these dearly departed souls of our relatives,
friends, neighbors, recounting the same old stories
as when once they were alive.
The stories still make them laugh.

So patient they are, these angels!
Beyond time, they wait at the gate
which opens onto the next world.
In the meantime, innocently,
within our nightly sleep,
we dream our usual deceptions one more night,
so sure that sleep is an unbreakable
habit and we will always wake again in the morning.
Between this world and the next
lies a narrow thread of a line,
and the gate opens and closes;
it closes and opens, but self-deception,
like the bright Sicilian sun, blinds us.

NNA PASSIATA NNI LA CHIAZZA

Duranti la notti silenziusa,
mentri nuautri d'Acquaviva dormimu a lettu,
nni la Chiazza Plado-Mosca c'e nna fudda
incredibili comu fossi menziornu!

Senza tuccari la strada,
camminanu abbraccettu,
le Bon' arme di nostri defunti:
Cari parenti, amici, paisani cca raccuntanu
le stisse storie 'nstu momentu e comu tannu
li fannu ridiri ancora.

Sunnu pasienti chissi anceli:
Sunnu libberi di tempu e cci
aspittanu a lu purtuni
cca apri a l'autru munnu.
Addurmisciuti, fratempu,
sunniamu nnuccentimenti
sonni ingannusi, e cridimu
cca chissu riposu notturnu
e nnu vizziu cca nuddu cci pu' livari!
Ppi forza, ogni matina sveliamu!
Fra ca e l'autra banna e nna cosa fina.
Lu purtuni apri e chiudi, chiudi e apri,
ma l'ingannu, comu lu suli luminosu sicilianu,
cci accica. Vidimmu nenti! Sappimu nenti!

We see nothing; we know nothing.
With eyes closed, we cannot watch
for that last day that looms in the distance:
First it appears like a fly
(black, tiny, innocuous, so far away)
but then too soon it grows quickly;

it becomes a train (black, powerful, approaching rapidly)
It cannot be stopped.
Its whistle is a serenade that lures the insomniac
and those who have run out of time.
Often there is not even a last moment
to steal a farewell kiss to take on the journey.

And in the Piazza Plado-Mosca
an incredible crowd gathers
as though it were afternoon!

Without touching the cobblestone street,
arm in arm, these dearly departed souls
recount their old stories.
Like kind hosts they stand solicitously at the gate,
awaiting the arrival of the next scheduled train.

Cu li occhi acussi chiusi,
nun putimu guardari chidda l'ultima iurnata
cca appari nna distanza: Prima comu nna musca--
niura, nica, e innocuu e poi doppu chidda musca
crisce troppu prestu e addiventa
nnu trenu-- niuru, potenti e avvicinnannu velucementi
Nun si pu' frenarlu.
La so friscata e nna canzuna, nna sirinata,
cca alletta chiddi cu l'insonnia, chiddi senza cchiu tempu.
Spissu mancu nnu vasuni pu' contrabbanneri cu tia!

*E nni la Chiazza Plado-Mosca c'e nna fudda incredibili
comu fossi menziornu! Senza tuccari la strada,
camminanu abbraccettu, le bonarme di nostri defunti:
Cari parenti, amici, paisani raccuntanu cose antiche.*

*Ospiti gentili,
si mittinu a lu purtuni,
attenninu lu prossimu trenu.*

SICILY

Not because you are maligned do I love you,
Underdog of the mainland,
a stone booted into the waters
of the Mediterranean;
the island where fools insist
crime was born once
when a young Sicilian groom avenged his bride
who died at the rapist's hand.

Sicily,
land where my fathers and mothers
sleep soundly,
I love you for your wisdom born of honor,
your loyalty to the millennia
buried in unwritten history,
your traditions carried down in strict lineage
that sidesteps death's
having its own way with words.

Sicily,
You can never die:
You who outlived the invading hordes
of every color; You who took from each
only the best and from it grew the wiser.
For you there is no death.
In my memories the old black-garbed widows
exchange deathbed-side stories;
children play soccer in the after-school sun;
Shadows tall in the piazza;
The church tower bell tolling the Angelus.

In my memories the young faces of pretty women
averting their eyes from the stare of L'Americano;
The bus ride over the hilly terrain noisy
with conversation; cobblestoned streets

(each a hero's name);
the spirit of my great grandfather
Giovanni still lauding the Garibaldi myth,
of my grandfather
Salvatore explaining why Mussolini
lost the war.

Sicily,
I love you because you are the haven,
the hideaway, the heaven
in the province of my heart,
the touchstone of all I learned as a child,
the voiceless cry of my ancestry.

Sicily,
I see you in the evening dusk,
a mild sirocco blowing the hair into your eyes,
your hair swirling across your dark complexion.
Again the taxi is honking outside.

Hurriedly we make promises:
We boast about how our love
is invincible.
"Sing a sad song"
keeps running through my mind.

Sicily
in the taxi's rearview mirror:
the quickly receding countryside,
a blurred panorama distorted by my tears.
Without a word,
without so much as turning
his eyes from the rocky road,
the Sicilian driver offers me a handkerchief.

SICILIAN TOWNS

I love the sound of Sicilian towns
Like Bolognetta, Sutera, and Canicattì.
To read on a map places like that:
Enna, Ragusa and Mussomeli.

My heart leaps high when I hear the cry
Of Bagheria, Messina, and Trapani.
I cannot explain the effect of these names
Like Ribera, Favara, Lercara Friddi

Each one is a song that moves me along:
Comiso, Catania, Castel Termini.
Each one a prize I give to my eyes:
Segesta, Sciacca, San Cataldo.

Castles and vines; Oh, Sicily mine!
Castel Buono, Marsala, Castroreale.
What could compare to the cool mountain air
Of Taormina, Marineo, and Corleone.

And where can the sea more bluer be
Than in Cefalù, Palermo, and Porto Empedocle?
But the village most dear, the one I most cheer,
Lu paisi about which I admit I'm most crazy:
Acquaviva Platani!
I love the sound of Sicilian towns!

SOUVENIRS

A bouquet of flowers
The stillness of the river
Don't let me forget

The tiny hands of an infant
A photo of my family
I will think of forever

Birds climbing the tall sky
A mandarin sun setting at night
I will remember them all

The sound of a heartbeat
And how love never dies
I tell you again   Don't let me forget

A white handkerchief for a cough
Sails white and lazy on a ship docked at port
I will hold them all dear in my memory

Those cobblestone streets
Where the boys are at play
Even the tears I have cried
All these souvenirs
I will take with me
Take with me forever!

RICORDI

Nu mazzu di sciuri
La calma di lu chiumi
Nun fammi scurdar'

Li mani nichi di un bambinu
Na fotografia di ma famigghia
Pensaró pi sempri

L'acceddi chi acchiananu fina ncelu
Lu suli mannarinu chi tramunta pi sira
Nni rigurdaró tutti

Nu battitu di cori
L'amuri chi nun mori mai
Ti dicu arriri: Nun mi fari scurdar'

Nu fazzulettu biancu pi la tussi
Veli bianchi e lagnusi di una navi a portu
Nni teniró cari nmemoria sempri

Chiddi stradi di petri
Unni iocanu li picciotti
Anche li lagrimi chi haiu chianciutu
Tutti sti ricordi nni portaró cu mia
Pi sempri mi li portaró!

SHORT STORIES

"...and for the second time since a lifetime ago, he was falling skyward like film spooling in reverse; like a fool walking his life backwards in a futile last-ditch effort to undo sin and stupidity..."

from: "With an Iron Hand"

CAST THE FIRST STONE

Giuvanni Zito waited for his attorney to speak, but Signor Amurosi said nothing. He didn't even raise his head from the notepaper sheet in front of him upon which he had pencil-drawn the scene of the murder. "No questions, your Honor," he said.

"No questions?" Giuvanni asked from the side of his mouth. "No questions?" he repeated. *"Signur' Avvucatu, ma, chi fa, scherza?"* ["Mr. Lawyer, what are you doing, fooling around?"] *"Salutammu lu munnu! Puru tu si contra di mia?"* [Let's say goodbye to the world! Even you are against me?"] But Amurosi, who looked as though he were going to reply, let his mouth curve into a smile instead. The prosecutor's voice summoned Giuvanni's attention back to the front of the courtroom where he was calling for still another townsman to take the oath and be word-whipped by his cleverness. Stefanu Nardo's voice was soft and almost pleasant, but in the fire of his black eyes cauldrons brewed.

"And what did Signor Zito mean when he

told you 'One more time he plays with my patience and he's a dead man'?" asked the prosecutor.

"Giuvanni is a good man, he would never—"

"Just answer the question Yes or No," interrupted Nardo. "Yes, he said that or No, he did not say that?"

"Yes, he said that. Yes."

The prosecutor nodded his balding head. "I see. And you are the defendant's—what? Brother-in-law? Cousin?"

"Brother," Luigi Zito whispered.

"A bit louder, Sir. The court cannot hear you. You are his...?"

"I am Giuvanni's brother," Luigi spoke too loudly this time.

Giuvanni trained his eyes on the Italian flag that served as backdrop to the judge's chair. The colors green, red, then white—he swam in them, pretended red was the blood boil that thieving bastard Riccobono had pulled him down into, pretended the green was the ocean on which he could float towards some far-off freedom, and the white, the sky or the ceiling of the next world's judgment court.

"Any questions?" the old judge asked

Giuvanni's attorney.

And once more Francpietru Amurosi shook his head. "No questions." Giuvanni watched the judge slap away a fly that must have flown in a halo around the old judge's head.

"Help me!" Giuvanni wrote on Amurosi's notepad. Then added in thick, bold lines: "Say something!" When his attorney made no attempt to write or speak any reassurance, Giuvanni looked back at the judge. He saw the fly had returned to annoy him. The judge this time had his hand shielding his forehead, then his cheek.

In the courtroom sat Giuvanni's young wife Enza, his father, his three brothers, the widow of Carmelu Riccobono, her grown sons and daughters. Two sides to every story, he told himself. One side wants me to live, the other, to die. I killed a man. No denying that. But how many times did I warn him? Go to the town hall and you'll find the property line that separated Riccobono's land from mine was clearly drawn. He had his parcel; I had my own, but every night while I slept, *chissu latru mi rubava na tanticchia una sira e nautra tanticchia la prossima sira.* [this thief robbed me a little one night and a little more the following night.]

The prosecutor was soft-speaking the courtroom now. He was reminding them that murder was murder; it didn't matter that Giuvanni had warned Riccobono to stop moving the property line. It did not matter that Giuvanni, after nights and nights of being made a fool, of being robbed, of losing meters of property, finally gave Riccobono one last warning: *"Fa arreri e t'ammazzu!"* ["Do it again and I'll kill you!"] Prosecutor Stefanu Nardo squinted his dark eyes diabolically and closed his summation with "There is no room for honor here. A man is insulted by another man. He cannot resort to murder in order to reclaim his honor. The verdict can only be 'Guilty as charged.' Giuvanni Zito must pay."

Then Giuvanni noticed his attorney lift his head, take from his top jacket pocket a small pebble and flick it towards the judge. Now Giuvanni saw the red-faced judge fidgeting in his chair, waving his hand, open-mouthedly gritting his teeth. Again Amurosi took from his pocket another pebble and flicked it like a cigarette butt too short to smoke. Once more the judge swatted the air in front of him. Like Nardo the prosecutor, his eyes were blazing. But Giuvanni's lawyer had more pebbles in the top pocket of his grey jacket so he flicked another into the face of the old judge. Then another.

The courtroom was silent. It was the judge's place now to call Attorney Amurosi to deliver his own summation. So far he had neither questioned nor cross-examined any witnesses, spoke no more than two or three sentences in his opening remarks, and made no objections to Stefanu Nardo's line of prosecution. It had seemed to Giuvanni that Amurosi had joined the enemy in delivering him a death sentence. He had sketched the death scene: he and Riccobono in their backyards under a quarter moon, Giuvanni's bare hands ready for action and old Carmelu, still egging him on, still challenging him with that cruel smile, those lying words, all that dishonor that left Giuvanni no choice but to murder him. And all the while Giuvanni watched justice play its hand against him, his own attorney, a distant cousin from Mussomeli, this Francpietru Amurosi, sat there tossing pebbles at the judge like some kind of madman, some fool who, of all times in Giuvanni's life, had lost his mind!

Suddenly the judge sprang to his feet in such a seemingly unprovoked wildness that nearly everyone in the courtroom flinched big-eyed and some even gasped. Shaking his fist, first the left, then the right, the old judge struggled with his tongue to spit out the words that boiled in his mouth. "You throw one more stone at me, whoever the son of a bitch out there, and I swear I'll kill you with my bare hands!"

It was Amurosi's turn now. He stood up and raised his hand. "I threw the pebbles, your Honor. One after the other. A pebble, then another pebble, then another and another. I watched your face with each pebble assault, your Honor. I watched the color of your complexion drain, then grow hot and dark. So I threw another pebble to see what would happen next. I could almost hear your heart pounding in anger. If I could read your mind, I would have known what you finally confessed: that if you had known who was throwing pebbles—or as you called them 'stones'—you would have murdered me. This is how strong your anger had become.

"Push a man, even an educated man, a judge like yourself, a professional man who knows the law as you do, and that man, whoever or whatever he is, will crack under the strain of such dishonor. Patience is a virtue, but how many of us have the patience of a saint? I beg indulgence, your Honor, but you don't. We have all seen evidence of that. I don't either.

Who in this courtroom has? So why should my client, Giuvanni Zito, a poor, uneducated farmer, be expected to go onnight after night seeing more and more of his property, for which he had slaved to own and keep, be taken from him? Why should Giuvanni Zito be any different from the rest of us? He warned Carmelu Riccobono morning after morning. But for whatever reason Riccobono would not desist. He continued, as I did, your Honor, throwing stones in the face of an honest man.

"I have nothing else to say. Find me someone now who would consider this an easy case of murder. What did the prosecutor say? 'Murder is murder'? What will you say now, Signor Nardo, about the judge? What if I had emptied my pocket of all the pebbles I had carried there and the judge were to have caught me throwing the ten or fifteen remaining and, losing his sanity for a moment, commenced to strangle me to death, the way my client strangled Carmelu Riccobono that evening he caught him redrawing the boundary between their properties? Would you, Signor Prosecutor, demand that the judge be found guilty of your easy 'murder is murder and that's that'?"

No one was surprised when the judge, back to

himself and in control of the courtroom, waved his hand and made his pronouncement. Giuvanni saw his life before his eyes flashing back to him. He was saved! He glanced down at Amurosi's notepad, saw where the attorney had scribbled a good likeness of the judge in his chair, swatting the pebbles that came flying towards him.

"Go," said said the judge.. "You're a free man."

MIRACLE MAN

What impressed the two of us back then was Uncle Tanoots teaching Gilda, our German Shepherd, to say "Mamma.' It turned out to be nothing supernatural, but to Rosa and me—impressionable grade-school kids brimming with faith—it was the most awesome miracle we'd ever seen.

"How'd you do that?" asked my little sister Rosa.

"Yeah, I chimed in, "how, Uncle Tanoots?"

"You got Gilda to say her first word! It's even better than last week," said Rosa, " when you made it rain by doing the Sicilian Rain Dance!" The old man laughed. It was the one thing Papa's old uncle did best.

Since that first day he had come to us from somewhere in Sicily, we had been taken in by him. He was funny, hilariously funny, something Papa never was in those early days. And he took time out to talk to us as if we were grownups. "You do you home-a-work?"

"Not yet, Uncle Tanoots. We'll do it later," Rosa said.

"Why you think they call it home-a-work?" he asked. We had an idea, but we knew his idea was better.

"Becausa now you home, you go do you work!" but as usual he said it all good-naturedly, not in a scolding way. Almost as if the word "homework" sounded humorous to him and he was testing it out on us. Soon enough he'd transform the tight, stern look on his face to loose, convulsive laughter. To Uncle Tanoots everything was funny.

Right now he was crouching down on the linoleum kitchen floor, watching Gilda try hard to bark or growl or make some canine sound, but all that would slide off her slobbering black tongue was the thin, mechanical voice of a baby calling its mother. "Mamma, Mamma, Mamma," said Gilda, bewildered by the alien human sound coming from her mouth. Those sad pathetic eyes played first on Rosa, then on me. Do something! Help your faithful dog Gilda. I got this big problem. I don't bark; I talk. Your great-uncle is ruining me!

My sister and I sat at the kitchen table, our schoolbooks all neatly covered in tan Acme shopping bags, sprawled over Mamma's linen tablecloth. It was homework time, but we couldn't bring ourselves to work; this was much too good to miss. What would Gilda say next? Would Uncle Tanoots teach her how to recite the Hail Mary in Sicilian or sing O Solo Mio"? But "Mamma, Mamma, Mamma" was all Gilda would say.

"A miracle!" Rosa said, her eyes looking up at the white, paint-peeling heaven that was our kitchen ceiling.

Uncle Tanoots shook his head, his smile as wide as the Strait of Messina. "'at'sa no miracle!" he said, then laughed some more. "When you wasa in school, Rosa, I giva the dog you littla doll for play. Buta the stupida dog she eata the doll! She eata inside-a the doll where littla recorda player say 'Mamma.' Mamma mia!" said Uncle Tanoots, "where you gonna find more stupida dog?"

Finally, he knelt down in front of the frightened Gilda, reached out, embraced her tightly around her quivering shoulders until the dog's face and his were muzzle to nose. Then Uncle Tanoots said some words in Sicilian—a prayer or a curse? With all his strength, his face turning the colors of the American flag, Uncle Tanoots squeezed Gilda tighter and tighter. All the while Gilda struggled, straining to break loose from this kneeling old lunatic. She wanted nothing in the world except to be left alone and speechless. But the old man wouldn't release her; he doubled his efforts, prayed, cursed, pulled the frantic dog even closer to his chest.

"Looks like he's trying to kiss Gilda," observed Rosa.

I thought about how Papa said his old uncle was a nutcase. Something about loose wires in his head; how years ago, when he was a young man, he flirted with a pretty girl named Monatello from his village, and her six brothers had come looking for him with lead pipes in the middle of the night. When they finally left poor Uncle Tanoots, his head looked like a huge busted tomato, blood everywhere. Nobody figured he'd survive. But he did. He lived, but all his dreams died. He would never go to medical school in Palermo. He'd never marry, never have children. Thanks to those Monatellos who played his head like an ugly drum, he would never become the healer, the miracle worker, he had always dreamed he'd be.

"He wants to come here?" asked my mother when the letter arrived from Sicily. "Here? To our home? Here?" she asked again. Then she chuckled. "You must be joking, right?" she asked my father while Rosa and I pinned our ears against the outside of their bedroom door. "We're getting a divorce, remember, Tony?"

I looked at Rosa; Rosa looked at me. Our faces asked the same question Mamma had asked Papa: You must be joking, right?

We heard the sound of the closet door slam. It was probably Papa; he did that when he was angry. He'd yell for awhile then walk away. After too much silence he said at last, "What's to joke? My uncle's all alone now that my mother's gone. For a few months he lives here. He needs—"

"That's the trouble with you!" my mother interrupted. It's always somebody in your family needs. What about your kids? Rosa and Paulie? Forget about me. Aren't they family? What about them?"

But Papa was not one to feed into Mamma's anger. True to form, he called it quits and kept quiet; he let her go on ranting about all the wasted years she had spent with him. "What about your promises to be caring and loving?" she harped. "What about a little goddamn consideration?" It was the only time

Rosa and I ever heard Mamma swear.

"Uncle Tanoots," Rosa pleaded, "let go of my dog! You're killing him!"

"Nonch' you worry, Rosa," said Uncle Tanoots through the few teeth he had left to clench. Through the spaces in his mouth, words whistled like tiny birds. "You joosta watch now," he said, and with that the "Mamma" contraption popped out of Gilda's mouth and sailed across the kitchen. Now Gilda was Gilda again. She tried out a bark. When it worked, she began barking in earnest. Nonstop. Loud and filled with relief, wounded pride, and downright anger.

When Uncle Tanoots raised his arm to show the dog he was still in charge, Gilda gave herself away by flinching, tucking her tail between her legs, then skulking off to the living room.

"When I wasa in Sicily, one time I heal four sicka pigs. They no wanna eat. They lie down ina the mud for die. The farmer he calla me. 'Doctor,' he say, 'You save-a my pigs?' Everbody know me in San Cataldo. I wasa the good doctor; Signor Miracle Man!"

Before Gaetano "Tanuzzu" Mendola--that was his real name--came to our home on Chalkstone

Road, Rosa and I were miserable. We were like spectators at a ping-pong match: first Mamma would scream at Papa, then Papa would scream back, then Mamma would scream—it went on that way until Papa would narrow his eyes to razor-thin slits, wave his hand to signal the fight was over and then walk away. All the while Gilda would bark at the two of them like she does at strangers outside who come too close to our house. It was not a happy life for us kids. We knew the day would come when their threats of divorce would stop being threats. We lived in fear that the fighting would never stop—No, worse! that the fighting would suddenly stop and the two of them would walk away from each other like two insulted enemies back to back, pacing ten steps for a duel, or like two gunslingers tired of threats, making final plans to shoot in all out.

In our misery Rosa believed Uncle Tanoots was really an angel sent from God to make all of us laugh again. To her he wasn't crazy at all. But she was only eight years old. What did she know! Me? At first, I figured he was a weird kind of babysitter—crazy, but not dangerous. He did funny things, even when it seemed he didn't intend them to be funny. In his head of loose wires he meant well: the world was in need of repair. He would say that over and over again as if we weren't listening the first twenty times.

"Why you fight?" he would hammer away at Mamma and Papa. "You calla this love? Nonch' you know millionsa poor people ina the world they starving withouta love? Anda you two throw love ina the garbage!"

Rosa and I would laugh. He sounded funny. The things he said were funny, but once I heard Mamma say to Papa, "Uncle Tanoots is a wise old man." And once I saw our parents go a whole day without so much as one unkind word to each other.

"Whata we need?" Uncle Tanoots said, out of the blue again, as usual. "Whata we need?" he repeated.

"About what?" asked Rosa, who always bit the bait of the old man's out-loud thinking.

Uncle Tanoots smiled, placed a loving hand on Rosa's little shoulder. "Whata we need?" he asked, as if the question was Rosa's, not his. Rosa nodded. "Vera little," he said. Then he walked away and sat in Papa's favorite chair.

Rosa followed him. "Tell me," she begged, tugging on the old man's arm.

Uncle Tanoots played hard to get. He

pretended to read the Italian newspaper Papa brought home to him every night. But Rosa was not one to ignore. By now she was climbing on the chair. "Tell me! Tell me what we need!"

Across the room Mamma raised her head from the novel she was reading, and Papa, sitting next to her for a change, raised his head, too. Not to be left out, I raised mine from the *Superman* comic in my hands.

"A family," said Uncle Tanoots. At first it sounded as though he were out on the limb of another tangent, some new message coming through the loose wires tangled up in his head. "It's alla you need in this life. "Family is ever'thing. You know why?" he asked Rosa.

"You know why?" he asked Papa.

"You know why?" he asked Mamma.

"You know why?" he finally asked me.

We all shrugged our shoulders. The way things were going in our family, who were we to even guess why family was everything!

Uncle Tanoots leaned back in Papa's chair till it creaked. He folded the newspaper twice and put it behind his head like a pillow. "You want a miracle?" he asked us. "You want Uncle Tanoots to go run and dance-a in the yard so tomorrow she rain? You wanta hear magic words? I shoulda snapa my fingers? You want a miracle?"

Then he stood and walked slowly towards Papa and Mamma. When he got to the couch where they sat, he leaned over, rested a bony hand on each of their heads like a man postured for a miracle. "Family," he said, eyes closed, voice trembling on the shaky edge of tears. "Family isa you miracle! Then he looked at them both and asked, "Will you believa? Before it'sa too late, will you believa?"

Then it got real quiet. Nobody spoke, not even the miracle worker. Rosa and I smiled. Uncle Tanoots had done it again: Papa and Mamma were holding hands!

NOBODY EVER CAME BACK...
EXCEPT PETRU SALAMONE

Jay Leno stands gloating in the green room. "Run out of material? Are you serious?" he asks one of the hangers-on from still another national gossip rag. "I switch on the news and find all I need to make folks laugh."

"Will they laugh tonight?" the reporter wants to know.

Leno glances up at the flashing on-air light, signaling two minutes to show time. Television Land will never forget this one, he tells himself. The big boys threw me the brass ring, and I'm gonna ride with it. Not Barbara Wa Wa. Not old Cronkite out of sleepy retirement. Not Sawyer. Not any of them! They picked me--Jay Leno. "You're the one he asked for," head honcho Bill Aronson had said. "The guy likes you, Jay. He thinks you're funny." So here he was, doing the show of a lifetime, on special early-night primetime no less. Johnny Carson, eat your heart out.

"Will they?" the reporter asks again.

"Oh, they'll laugh all right," says Leno. "The

guy's been dead for almost a year. Now he's back to tell it all on my show. You want funnier than that? Ok, how's this? He's not a famous dead actor or one of those departed televangelists back from the next world to pitch one more 'Save your soul. Send money.' He's not a limelighter, nobody you or me or anyone would recognize. He's an old Sicilian bricklayer named Petru Salamone. Come on. Give me a break!"

Now the light is flashing in earnest. the countdown has begun and Jay Leno straightens the tie knot of his red and black Pierre Cardin as he lumbers down the long corridor towards the *Tonight Show* stage. From another room his guest Petru Salamone exits and follows beside one of the show's producers.

The usual cue of applause out of the way, Leno smiles, then begins his monologue. "No, folks, I'm not the guy who's dead. And hopefully my jokes will pass the 'breathe-on-a-feather' test some of you E.R. Clooneys out there might care to administer.

[Laughter.] "I mean, do I look dead? And if I were dead, would I come back to the show I died on?

"So what's in the news? Who cares, right? I mean, who can top our special guest tonight? Who cares if Monica Lewinsky is upset after finding out the government is not going to pay her all that overtime. Who cares if Kenneth Starr was voted "Most Likely to Bust Chops" back in high school. Who cares if President Clinton quit smoking cigars and the U.N. today drew up a formal declaration of war against Iraq, and Saddam who's hiding out somewhere in the Bronx says he's not complying, and El Niño just met up with La Niña and the two of them plan to go on this rampage and drown the Alamo and trash all the Taco Bells in Texas.

"Do we have news or what. But all of it is a drop in the bucket next to the biggest news anywhere. The news of Petru Salamone. 'Man kicks bucket and then returns to kick ass!' How's that for a headline? I read somewhere that the clone scientist Dr. Seed is taking full credit for Petru's return. Yeah, he insists our guest is a clone he made while Seed was on vacation in Palermo several years ago. This was long before Seed turned to sheep." [Laughter.] "Now Seed is going to seed. Okay, okay, I guess you've heard about all you can take, so let's get on with the show."

The camera follows Leno back to his desk where he sips something from a cup, and then waves his hand to the guest across from him. "Back by popular demand and a king-size miracle, Petru Salamone! Let's hear it!" Leno says, clapping his hands and motioning the audience to do likewise. Not quite understanding, Salamone joins in applauding, which starts the audience laughing again. Feigning anger, Leno darts a stern eye at him and says, "Now wait a second. I do the comedy around here. I'm Leno; you're Lazarus. Got that?"

Petru, shaken by Leno's outburst, sits and fidgets with the items on Leno's desk: accidentally he snaps a pencil in half, then spills some of the contents of the cup. When Petru pulls his hand back, Leno's face gets in the way and gets slapped. By now the audience is roaring. Leno leaps out of his chair, makes a major production of skirting around his desk, pulls Salamone up by the lapels of his charcoal-gray suit, lifts the five-foot-three-inch Sicilian half a foot off the couch. What makes the scene so Laurel-and-Hardyesque is that Salamone is missing the humor in it. Sicilian humor is rarely physical. Slapping one's forehead or flicking the thumb outwardly from the underside of one's chin or making unmentionable arm-flexing gestures are never meant to be humorous. Salamone defends himself by flailing his arms and yelling, *"Basta! Basta!"* ["Enough! Enough!]

"Ladies and Gentlemen, I think I just heard the Sicilian word for 'Uncle,' says Leno. "Or is Signor Salamone reliving his salad days as a waiter in Palermo's Famous Pasta House on the Paisan' Strip? You give up, Petru? Had enough?" Leno releases the old Sicilian. Gently he eases him back onto the couch.

Salamone is visibly trembling, his swarthy complexion pasty, nearly white. But then Leno offers him a handshake, and Petru calms down enough to smile nervously.

"You okay, Petru?" Petru nods. "Ready to tell the world how you made it back? I mean, you were dead, for crying out loud. Last you remember you were up on a scaffold laying bricks on a Palermo high-rise when the wall above you collapsed on your head. You were crushed. Thousands of falling bricks. You were splattered down there on the sidewalk. Okay, that sounds like dead to me. Then what happened? You were buried. Nothing unusual there. Would you tell us the rest of the story? Just walk over there," Leno says.

Petru Salamone, seventy years old and recently deceased, but none the less for wear, shuffles his feet   towards the spotlight while the orchestra begins the fanfare of "When the Saints Go Marching In."

Self-consciously he stands there in the white circle of the spotlight, staring out at the audience. Without waiting for the music to stop, he begins to speak. "My name isa Petru Salamone."

The music stops. He clears his throat. "Petru Salamone from Palermo, Sicily. For many year I was bricklayer.   I builda houses, make a money for Salvatrice my wife, for my daughtersa Carmela and Mariana. We live gooda life. We no starve. It was gooda livin'."

From off the stage we hear the voice of Leno. "Tell them about your gooda dyin', Petru."

"The line betweena live anda die isa vera thin. When we alive, we no give a much attench' to dyin'. Maybe we think we gonna live forev'. We make a jokes like Mr. Leno. Evera thing funny. Evena the grave.

"I no remember when I crossa the line. They say the wall she fall on a me, but I remember feela joosta one brick befo' I close a my eyes. When I opena them, I was in a de nexta life."

Again Leno's voice: "You saw Peter at the

Pearly Gates?"

Petru smiles, shakes his head. "I see my littla sister Teresa. She die when I was boy. 'Petru,' she say, *Benvinutu* [Welcome]! to Paradise!" We embrace I aska her. "I am dead?"

"*No, caru frati* [dear brother], you are alive now! Walk with me," she tella me. All a once I see *Gesu Cristu* [Jesus Christ]! He smile and say, "*Benvinutu, Petru. Finalmenti si arrivatu* [Welcome, Petru. Finally you've arrived.].

"Gesu, you speak Sicilian?"

"I speaka de language newcomers speak. Sicilian, Spanish, Polish, English. Whatever makes it easier you firsta day here."

Again Leno: "What does Jesus look like, Petru? Beard, sandals, long hair, blue eyes?"

Petru's eyes fill with tears. Too emotional to trust himself to speak, he waits, then tries a reply, but he fails.

"Don't die on me now, Salamone," says Leno's voice, but no one laughs.

Finally Petru says, "I no have-a words. No way I can describe Him. But my soul find comfort in Hisa voice. I was no more afraid. And how brighta wasa Gesu! Brighter than the Palermo sun, but He no blind me. For the firsta time in my life, I coulda see mo' clear than everbefo'."

"So how did you get back here? "Tell the truth now. Was it a near-death experience?"

"It wasa no near, Mr. Leno. It wasa the real thing. I die, I see heaven, anda Gesu He senda me back to talk ona TV."

"Just once? Or are you here to take my job"

"Joosta thisa one time and then I go backa home."

"Palermo?"

"Paradiso."

"And what does Jesus want you to tell the largest viewing audience in the history of the world?"

Petru sighs, like a man physically unprepared to support the burden he's been ordered to shoulder. At one point he closes his eyes. When he opens them, everyone expects to see tears again, but Petru's dark eyes are dry, set hard and piercing. They stare into the camera, into the depths of every viewer waiting on this message from heaven.

A drum roll begins, but Petru shakes his head in disapproval, and it stops. Not even Jay Leno will fill the silence now. The world waits.

"'Why me?' I aska. 'Why Petru Salamone?

Why senda me?' I aska Gesu. 'Go back, Petru. Tella them to repent. Tella them about heaven. How life on earth she'sa short. Tella them love one another anda repenta.'"

"That's it?" asks Leno. "This is the message of all time? You came all the way from heaven to tell the world 'Repent'?"

The camera focuses now on a speechless Jay Leno. The camera pans the audience where, like a stilled frame, no one moves. The band too is silent.

When the camera returns to center stage, the spotlight is empty of Petru Salamone. Only his final word, whispering over and over again from another world: "Repenta. Repenta. Repenta. Repenta."

NONNU

I don't remember after all these years. My mother had gone upstairs to visit Jamie's folks or somebody in the building. Or my mother had gone to morning mass at All Saints. The apartment was empty except for my old grandfather in his bed, as usual. And of course there was me, running my little wooden tractor hard across the kitchen floor.

At first I hadn't heard him call me, I was so busy with the tractor, adding my own mimicking truck sounds to the pounding of the toy. Finally, almost annoyed, I let myself be interrupted and I tramped into his bedroom.

"Ancilu," he called to me. "Ancilu." He was the only one in the world who called me that. My name was really Angelo.

"Nonnu?" I asked because that was the name my mother said to call him because "Grandapa isa too 'mericanu!" "*Nonnu*" meant "Grandpa" in Sicilian.

He sounded funny, not at all like Nonnu's voice. Had I heard it in another room or had I closed my eyes to his crooked mouth, I am sure even now that I would not have recognized it. The calling of my name did not ring with the promise of one more funny story from Nonnu's story collection. It promised nothing I could feel good about.

The small cot creaked as Nonnu, trembling all over, extended his gnarled fingers to me. I kept my distance, just enough that his fingers could not touch me. With each pitch of his hand toward me, sweat would spray me and I'd flinch as if burned. What was happening to my Nonnu? To his eyes rolling up and down. To his lips coated with a whiteness like slime across which his tongue like a lizard's flicked feverishly. To his brown eyes fluttering madly, staring at me but somehow not seeing me, not seeing me at all.

"Nonnu, what's the matter?" Again his shaking hand clawed hopelessly at my shirt. Then it tore away a button that made my chest sore.

"Please don't do that," I said.

Inside of me the crying would soon enough burst forth and I'd be the baby Nonnu always told me not to be. *"Hai sei anni, Ancilu. Nun chianciri chiù. Ormai si nu omu."* ["You're six years old, Angelo. Don't cry anymore. You're a man now."]

"Anci...Ancilu," he whispered. Cautiously I moved closer to him but heard only the wheezing rise and fall of the old man's chest. No words. A dry gargle from his throat. A mumbling. A mute beating of his lips, the pink tongue darting in and out, the glazed eyes. The gargle again like a snoring out of sleep.

Man or no man, I was six years old and so I started to cry. God! There were too many sounds! A menagerie of unexplained horrors. "Tell me, tell me," I screamed, and Nonnu tried to tell me because his white lips were jerking convulsively up and down and the hand I had held so many times before was an ugly, wet, white claw.

"*Dimmi, Dimmi,*" [Tell me, tell me,] I was screaming now. Nonnu answered but he did not speak. Instead came a gargle, a wheeze, a growl, a thrashing of lips and a waving of his hand.

"*Sugnu iu.* [It's me] —Ancilu. *Nun mi fa scandari.* [Don't scare me. I'm afraid.*"] His claw clamped itself once more to my shirt. It tugged and trembled. "Please, Nonnu," I begged him, trying oh so hard to break away.

"You're hurting me. *Mi fa chianciri.* [You're making me cry!*"]

Then the trembling hand fell limp onto the cot. Free, I backed away and nearly stumbled to the farthest part of the room. Nonnu's glassed marble eyes, wet with tears, followed me. The mouth opened and closed like a fish pulled out of water. No words. The hand was clawing again but at nothing but air. Air. I needed air because the fear of it all was making me light-headedly weak. This was new to me and it only made me all the more afraid.

I began to scream. "Stop! You better stop now! You stop, Nonnu. Please stop!" I brushed away the hot tears that bubbled from my eyes. Inching forward, I moved a safe distance from his cot. "You hurt me. You're making me cry. You don't say anything." We were both too old to cry, but we were crying. "It's me, Nonnu. Can't you see it's Ancilu?" I stood there and listened to the ugly, heavy up and down breathing of the old man I loved. The man, the room, the cot. All part of my favorite world and they were conspiring against me, melting into one nightmare that rooted me now to the floor like the demon power of a bad dream.

Then I heard my name again, not like the many times before this hell began. Not like the times it rang of promised tales. Not even like the short world ago when I collided the wooden tractor into the kitchen chair, stood up, and walked into this room to answer the calling of my name.

In a voice strong enough now to sound like my Nonnu, he said, "Ancilu," and I took this as a sign everything would be all right now. I nearly dashed to his bedside.

"Yes, yes, Nonnu. It's me, Ancilu." So close was I now that my head nearly rested on the boniness of his hot, wet, pajamaed chest. Nonnu was doing that again with his lips. A cold shiver fanned my ear, coursed my spine, because the trembling old man was popping air bubbles of saliva out of closed lips.

Then he said, *"Aiutami. Aiutami."* [Help me. Help me."] And I watched the world's oldest man ask me, the world's most frightened, confused six-year-old boy to "Help me please!"

Barely audible, the words echoed through the room. This was my loving grandfather pleading with me. The same old man who had kissed my splintered finger, with a lion's fierce growl chased the pain away, warned it never to come back. The old friend who once made me laugh so hard and for so long without let-up I wet my pants. Old Nonnu who...The cold, clammy hand in a last appeal touched my face. I screamed. Turned. Ran from the room. Tripped over the door jamb. Got up. Raced through the kitchen, the apartment door, down the stairway. My mother is probably upstairs, I remember telling myself, but I'm running the other way. Two, three steps at a time down those three flights.

Shaking and panting, I stopped finally at the basement door. It was open. Again, two, three steps at a time, in a blind panic, I ran down those basement stairs, darted into the darkness of an unlit coal bin and hid there.

Upstairs in hell something was happening. Whatever it was I was convinced I'd never leave the dark unless I could close my eyes and wish myself to wake up to another morning filled with Nonnu's laughter. That seemed unlikely, so I would sleep atop the hard, lumpy filth of the blue-black coal, become hilariously clown-dirty with coal dust and be without my Nonnu to find my face funny enough to laugh at.

"Pirchí m'hai abbannunatu? [Why did you abandon me?"] It was Nonnu's voice but it wasn't real. It was his voice playing tricks in my mind. I tried to think it out of me, but then inside my mind he kept talking anyway, *"Pirchí t'ammucci da mia?"* [Why do you hide from me?]

"Nonnu! Nonnu!" I said in the darkness. "I am afraid!" And in my head, I could see him making those horror-mask faces and those scary noises, shaking squeals into the cot springs, saying in a voice weak but cold enough to chill me, *"Avia bisugniu di tia. Pirchí mi lassasti?"* [I needed you! Why did you leave me?"]

I pushed my back deeper into the coal heap. Who was that old man upstairs? I wondered. You don't become somebody else, chase a funny old man out of his bed and steal his place. Where was my Nonnu? So often I had said to him, "If you ever need me, will you call?" He promised me he would. And while I played with that stupid wooden tractor, he had called. Didn't he say, "Help me"? Didn't that mean he was calling me?

"Where are you, Nonnu? *Ti vugliu beni!* [I love you!] Please come back." But even as I said it, I knew it was no use.

***

"Ancilu? Ancilu?" Someone was calling me. I opened my eyes from what I believed a short sleep.

"Are you down here?" said the voice. Then a pounding on the coal bin door. There was nowhere to hide. Like an executioner's drum the pounding grew louder, more menacing. My hand in my mouth, I bit down hard on my fingers, tasting the foul soot.

Once Nonnu had said God gets lonely in heaven and He calls people to go up there and live with Him. I had run away; I had left Nonnu unprotected from the snares of a lonely God.

Finally the knocking stopped. I prayed God was on the other side, lonely for me and not for Nonnu. "I made a mistake," he would say to me. It's not the old man I want; it's you." But it was my father's brother, Uncle Carlo, who opened the coal bin door. Behind him was my mother, crying. "Nonnu," said my uncle, "is in heaven now, kid."

And though it has been so many many years since that black Brooklyn morning, I still remember screaming at both of them, "He's not in heaven! He's dead! Nonnu is dead!"

Then, while my mother reached down into the blue-black darkness to embrace me and cry into my shoulder, I told her I was sorry. "Don't make me go upstairs, Mama," I begged. "He needed my help, but I ran away. Please, Mama! He tried to tell me something, but I was afraid."

She breathed in a long sigh, lifted my chin so our wet eyes met in the basement's half-light, and she kissed my cheek.

"*Ancilu, to nonnu ti salutá cu stu vasu.* Angelo, you Nonnu he give a you thisa kiss goodbye."

AN INTERVIEW WITH ARCHIMEDES

No book about Sicilians would be complete without mention of Sicily's favorite son Archimedes. However, not content with simply mentioning that renowned mathematician, engineer, and physicist, the author of *A Family of Sicilians...* tracked him down by spending the better part of 1997 running search ads in both Greek and Sicilian newspapers and then hiring a missing-persons detective from Siracusa, Sicily. No one responded to the ads except an impostor named Archimopolis, proprietor of The Lazy Zeta Diner in downtown Athens. And as for the Sicilian missing-persons detective, he was found months later feeblemindedly wandering the streets of Messina, babbling that he himself was the great Archimedes!

As luck would have it, an anonymous e-mail to the author contained Archimedes' URL. The genius had figured a way onto the World Wide Web where he was teaching calculus to bedridden octagenarians who'd never made it to senior year of high school. From the Elysian Fields where he had been resting since his death in 212 B.C., Archimedes was again in his glory. Here then is the Archimedes interview conducted by the author via the Net during the month of June 1998.

Q: A Greek in a book of Sicilians?

A: My father—Phidias by name—was Greek. I was born in Sicily.   In Siracusa. Long before the Arabs, the Normans—even before the Romans.

Q: Did you speak Greek or Sicilian?

A: Greek, of course, but I did understand enough of the vernacular to get by. A favorite expression of mine was *"Ma chi fa—babbia?"* which I'd often use at the marketplace when a "Siggie"—that's new slang for Sicilian—tried to overcharge me. It translates "What are you trying to do—rip me off?" Those native Sicani and Siculi folks would steal your eyeballs!

Q: In 800 B.C. the Ancient Greeks founded Siracusa, Catania, Messina, Gela-- a string of colonies, with Siracusa eventually taking over all of Sicily. How did you fit into the scheme of things? Local poor boy makes good?

A: Good Zeus, no! My father was an astronmer. We had more drachmas than we could spend.

Q: Silver coins?

A: Gold coins too. I never went without. I wore expensive clothes, ate the best foods. I even had a lifetime membership at the most exclusive bath house in all of Siracusa: "*Lu Spazziu*" ["The Place"], which later we simply called the "spa."

Q: Speaking of the baths--

A: Here it comes. "Tell me about your famous experiment where the idea came to you in the bathtub." Right?

Q: Something like that. History tells us that a friend of yours, Hiero, the king of Siracusa, asked if you would solve a puzzle for him. The king had given a local goldsmith enough gold to make him a crown of specified size and weight. But when Hiero got the crown, he suspected all that glittered in it wasn't gold. He wanted you to prove the jeweler had pulled a fast one. Is that

accurate so far?

A: So I figured it out for him and the thieving goldsmith was executed.

Q: You figured it out in your tub, then jumped up, ran naked down the streets of Siracusa, screaming "Eureka! Eureka! I found it! I found it!"

A: Pardon me for laughing. That's ridiculous! Who peddled that tale—those idiot historians from Rome, Pliny? Plutarch? Here's what really happened. Yes, I was in my tub. I liked going there to think. I was always a thinker. I'd draw geometric figures, especially circles, in the dirt, in the dust, even on the surface of my bath water! Now here's one you modern Sicilians would appreciate: after a bath I would anoint myself with olive oil and trace figures in the oil on my bare skin! Today you'd call it "Obsessive-Compulsive Disorder," but in my day the Greeks called it "Genius." And I read everything I could get my eyes on, even the labels on burlap bags of wheat! And while I'm in a confessing mood, I also had a fondness for rubber duckies.

Q: Rubber duckies?

A: I couldn't take a bath without one. So it happened one day I noticed that when I pushed down on Darius the Rubber Duck, the amount of water that overflowed my tub was proportional to the amount of Darius the Duck that was submerged. I called that discovery "Dunking Darius," but I understand history preferred calling it "Archimedes Principle." What also occurred at that point was that Darius ruptured underwater and fizzled itself flat. What I did then was jump out of that tub—yes, naked!—and cry at the top of my lungs, "Confound it! Confound it! I'm no streaker! I'm no streaker!" as I raced down the Siracusan streets in search of "Toys 'R Theodus," the leading purveyor of bath toys. Of course, I was frightened of being arrested. Streaking was a capital offense; it was enough to have me done in, mathematician nothwithstanding.   I could be subjected to my own "principle": submerged in boiling water and made to displace my own skinless weight!

Q: **That's quite interesting, Archimedes. And here is another quote you allegedly made about another of your discoveries, or inventions: the compound pully or perhaps the lever. "Give me a place to rest my lever and I will move the earth."**

A: What a crock! If this is how blatantly false history is recorded, maybe we ought to stop writing it down. What I actually said was, "Give me a place in Taormina to rest from being clever and the earth can go rotate without me."

Q: **Your accomplishments boggle the mind, Sir.**

A: I also invented calculus to the dismay of 1,800 years of high school math students. I helped the war effort by inventing weapons. Can you believe it? That same Greek Hiero begged me to help Siracusa hold back the advancing army of Romans, led by General Marsellus. That was another story.

Q: As it turned out, that was the end of the story?

A: It was the end of me. Even geniuses, great thinkers, master mathematicians, eventually go the way of the Elysian Fields. I was an old man of seventy-five who foolishly thought he'd one day die quietly in his tub. But it wasn't in the stars.

Q: What happened?

A: Despite my inventions: giant catapults hurling half-ton rocks, large cranes able to lift ships into the air and dash them against the mountainside, huge mirrors to blind advancing soldiers—despite it all, Marsellus, after eight long months, entered the gates while most citizens of Siracusa were attending a night festival to Artemis. Siracusa fell shortly after. Did I know? I was—you guessed it!—drawing circles in the dust of battle. Roman soldiers were plundering everywhere.

Suddenly one of those soldiers stepped on my work and ground his boot into my designs. "Come with me, Greek!" he says. Well, I am so angry I could spit. "You're standing on my circles, Geek!" I reply, and with that, he draws his sword and slays me. Even Marsellus comes to my funeral pyre. Crowds of fellow Sicilians arrange themselves in very neat circles around my pyre to bid me farewell. Would you believe that after the ceremony my spirit could not resist kneeling down in my own ashes and drawing some more circles?

Q: How do you pass your retirement days? Are you still into geometry?

A: The Elysian Fields. Now why did it sound so interesting when they talked about it in the Greek temples? Boring is the only word that comes to mind that you will not have to edit out of your book. Nearly 2,000 years here. Even a genius could go mad! How do I spend my time?   I sit in the piazza, discoursing with Isaac Newton, Descartes, thinkers like that. We reminisce in an outside cafe. We each take turns treating the rest to espressos and pastry. Stirring sugar into my espresso, I lose myself to memories while the spoon draws black concentric circles along the perimeter of my cup.

Q: Well, Archimedes, it was a pleasure conversing with you on the Internet. I am proud to include you within my family of Sicilians.

A: Eureka, huh? Eureka! After all these centuries, it doesn't sound like Greek to me at all.

WITH AN IRON HAND

Manucomiu. Manucomiu. The word cut through him like a sword. Madhouse. How many months now? Or were they years? He couldn't be certain. Not of anything. When he was a boy, up till the moment he stood outside the boarded entrance to Coffaro, one of the two rock-salt mines outside the village of Cammarata, he thought he knew about time: it ticked on the huge clock high in the tower of Duke Luigi Oliveri's palace. It was measured in seconds, minutes, hours, days, weeks—years! He had heard the old men in the Piazza Marina reminisce about how the exploits of Giuseppi Garibaldi delivered glory days to all Italy, including his village of Acquaviva Platani nestled in the mountains of central Sicily.

It was all about time remembered and time forgotten. Now, May 1900, he sat hunched over, peering out the slit of a curtained window that barred the outside Palermo afternoon from him because he was too dangerous to walk free out there. Too insane. Too much a madman. A high wire circus fool who tottered between two worlds: neither wanted him and both wanted him silenced. In one world he was a prisoner here in this 1900 madhouse; in that other world of 1944 he would have been a dead man in the fields outside Rome, brutally done away with. Buried. Forgotten.

"*Signur' Ministru*," spoke the attendant named Marcu. "*Senti friddu? Nnu mantellu?*" No, he thought to himself, I am not cold; I have no need of a cloak. And my name? You call me "Sir Minister," but what of Cosimu? Why not who I am: Cosimu Lipani! He kept his dark eyes riveted on the ragged seam of the curtain where sunlight rode motes of bobbing dust. Marcu sighed. "*Comu vuoi. T' aiutu e mi punisci cu lu silenziu. Marcu parla cu Marcu.*" ["As you wish. I help you and you punish me with silence. Marcu talks with Marcu."]

But the man was not a bad fellow; he reached over and pulled back the curtains. "Out there, Sir Minister, is the true madhouse," he said good-naturedly. It was hard to dislike Marcu when the rest of the attendants—sadists every one!—physically maltreated Cosimu, withheld his meals, used him as fodder to spark their cruel humor. "Out there, Sir, walk the ones who manage to pace themselves two steps ahead of the net. Landlords, peasants, government clerks, even the priests who boast one foot out there and one foot in heaven! I say instead one foot in this madhouse hell and the other Foot—who can say. The other hell perhaps. You who insist you are Cosimu Lipani, are in truth one of the *Disgraziati*—the unlucky fools—who got caught. And once you enter these unholy walls, life is over for you. Like the damned. Did you hear the passersby shouting on the sidewalks again last night?

"Four months into the new century and still now and then someone celebrates the merriment with too much wine. *Li strati affudati di buttani e chiddi chi li cercanu.* [The streets crowded with whores and those who seek them out.] The first year, 1900, and you are here without cause for celebration. Without even words to spit at me, *Signur'.* What are you thinking? It is May. Three months already and still you choose not to speak beyond the babble of those first few days."

For a fleeting second he hooked his dark eyes with Marcu's, then turned away. Words? What good would they do. Where might he go to find the appropriate ones to break his silence, to which, like a monk's vow, he had so far remained true? He felt himself smile. There are no words, dear Marcu, spit out or otherwise. My thoughts remain best hidden. The words that would escape me God Himself would not believe!

Outside on the street a trio of lads boisterously tried to keep a waist-high wheel upright by hitting it into a rolling balance with sticks nearly a meter long. Sarbaturi, Vannu, Antò! His childhood companions: how those laughing boys resembled them! In Acquaviva Platani, on this very day, it would not surprise him if those three friends of his were now playing that same old game of teasing the girls in Maistra De Vittori's class or pilfering caramels from the tobacco shop in the piazza, the one owned by "Un Occhiu," [*"One Eye"*] Cosimu's Great-uncle Caloriu Fontana. How to explain it to Marcu! On the one hand, my young twelve-year-old companions are at home in Acquaviva Platani three months after my disappearance, resigned I won't be coming back. On the other hand, I, an old man of fifty-six, have lived a lifetime somewhen else! A man old enough to be the father of his own parents!

You see, Marcu, why words fail me? To makes sense of madness? The handiwork of demons? What would it serve to tell my story? It would not open these doors for me. If anything, my confession would seal my sentence here. It would settle once and for all: I am where I belong.

February 1900. He no longer remembered much about that day. Sometimes memories flashed in vivid nightmares, a sleep time when he'd recall too much of that early Saturday afternoon. Even the dark blue knickers he wore. The white shirt handed down from his brother Pippinu. The black shoes—once Pippinu's too!—a size too large, the leather lashed by the brambles on Cosimu's nearly vertical hike up the side of *Lu Salinaru*, the salt mine, where he had no business at all.

Hiding in those same bramble bushes, he watched the miners in one of the rock archways hammer and pick at the rock salt. In nightmare he even felt the heat of the treacherous Sicilian sun burning down on him.

Then Cosimu heard the miners shouting curses as he raced towards another entrance, this one nearly all boarded up: "*Vietato entrare. Pericoloso.*" ["Do not enter. Dangerous!"] Daredevilingly, sidling himself against the slats of splintering wood, he eased his small-boy body inside the condemned mine.

All this he had forgotten later on, except what he had culled piecemeal from the frames of so many projecting strips of recurring nightmares.

Once inside the mine, heart pounding in a twelve-year-old's bravado, he raced more deeply into the quasi-darkness until he no longer heard the voices of the miners outside. He could not turn back now. He'd take it a cautious step at a time. His hand tapped the cold walls like a blind man. It was a simile that would prove less figurative than he'd hope for. Then he stumbled. His fingers fluttered for the safety of the wall, but the wall was out of reach. Cosimu braced himself as the ground flew up, it seemed, to bruise him, but instead there was no ground, only Cosimu in mid-air, falling through what he suspected might have been wide cracks beneath him. Like loose change, he tumbled in a fall that seemed to him abysmal. Nevertheless, he stiffened for impact that would surely kill him, but it never came.

Of his horrendous salt mine ordeal, most remained a blur in consciousness. But what he did remember, and clearly so, was finally opening his eyes and finding himself on his feet. Alive.

It was still afternoon, but the Cammarata Mountain was gone. Before him, instead, a loud procession of people, mostly men, filled the streets of a city he first surmised was either heaven or hell.

Suddenly he heard the agonizing scream of a tortured man.

When he looked down at the hairiness of his huge arms, he realized it was he who had screamed. Apparently in the din and commotion of all that pedestrian traffic, no one had heard or cared. Cosimu touched his bearded face. *"Bedda Matri! Nun sugnu nu picciottu chiù!"* ["Blessed Mother! I am not a boy anymore!"] Still, the tears stinging his cheeks came easily.

"Join us, Brother," someone said as Cosimu leaned dizzyingly against the streetlight. "A new day is dawning." He took Cosimu by the arm and hustled him into the flow of the moving crowd. This will end soon, Cosimu told himself. All nightmares do. Patience. Patience. Twelve-year-old boys do not fall inside salt mines and rise up men in strange cities.

"Where is this?" he asked the man older than Cosimu's new self by at least ten years. "What city?" The stranger in the black shirt gripped Cosimu's arm and laughed heartily.

"Look around you," he said. "History will mark this day!" Cosimu noticed everywhere men in that same black shirt. A nightmare. Of course, black shirts.

"Today we march 20,000 strong, and back there," he began, throwing a thumbed fist over his shoulder, "another 30,000 wait on the outskirts of Rome."

"Rome?"

"The seat of government since the first Caesar. We fascists will take them all by the seat of their pants!"

"Rome?" he asked again. "*Sugnu Sicilianu.*" ["I am a Sicilian."] He could hardly understand the Italian with which he had been struggling in Maistra De Vittori's class only the day before when he was twelve and safe in Acquaviva Platani where Sicilian was spoken, not the high tongue of Dante's Italy.

"*Il Fascismo è per tutti gl'Italiani, anche per voi Siciliani. Benito Mussolini sarà il nostro salvatore!*" ["Fascism is for all Italians, even you Sicilians. Benito Mussolini will be our savior!"]

"My name is Cosimu Lipani," he finally said, offering the stranger a trembling right hand. What could he say of fascism or of Benito Mussolini. They signified nothing. He knew neither. Where he came from in Sicily it was 1900 time. Here in Rome—it was—it was what? Dream time? Somewhere in a future chimera where black was the color of revolution, and boys became men without paying the price of time?

Cosimu waited for him to take his proffered hand, but the stranger used his left hand to grasp Cosimu's right.

"Roberto Donatelli," he said.

At that moment Cosimu noticed the man's gloved right hand hidden under the black cuff of his sleeve. At least he thought it was a glove—a black one, an idiosyncrasy perhaps or a fascist thing like a secret society handshake. All he could think of was the story his maternal grandmother Nanna Cardinale once told him. "*Na bota c'era nu omu tindu chi avia na manu di firru. Vuliva mitteri na donna-- na principessa!-- ni lu furnu addrumattu. Idda avia nu cavaddu cu lu nnomu 'Ronellu.' Prima di chist' omu la ghittà nndintra, idda chiamà pi lu so cavaddu: 'Ronellu! Ronellu! Ronellu!'"* ["Once upon a time there lived an evil man with an iron hand who wanted to hurl a woman— a princess!—into a lit furnace. The woman had a horse named 'Ronellu.' Before the man pushed her into the furnace, she called her horse: 'Ronellu! Ronellu! Ronellu!'"]

Cosimu held the stare too long. When finally he raised his eyes, Donatelli was smiling at him. "Does it scare you?" he asked Cosimu. "In your Sicilian Paisi—your little village—have you seen one

before? Cosimu shook his head, then allowed himself
a more attentive look at the five-fingers of metal.
Donatelli straightened out his right arm, raised the
cuff, eased his iron hand out from its sleeve. "It
replaced the one I lost in 1895. Bloody Abyssinia.
You might say it's what Benito and I share in
common. That singular thing that makes of us more
than Black Shirts. *Fratelli*! Brothers! Two men like
brothers wielding iron hands!"

Grandmother Cardinale had said, "*Tri boti
chiamà: 'Unni si, caru cavaddu miu?' Dopu vini stu cavaddu,
pigghià l'omu cu la manu di firru e lu ghittà ni lu furnu e iddu
morì abbrusciatu.*" ["Three times she called: 'Where are
you, dear horse of mine?' Then this horse of hers
came, took the man with the iron hand and knocked
him into the furnace where he was burned alive."]

The nightmare never ended. The miners did
not find him on the mine floor and carry him
unconscious onto the hillside. He did not wake up to
Dr. Camalò's black bag or his father's reprimanding
voice or his mother's weeping. In an inexplicable leap
across time, Cosimu Lipani traversed twenty-two
years in the blink of a frightened eye, his childhood
years and his young adulthood, swallowed in a
heartbeat. And as for Acquaviva Platani, he had

likewise leaped across space into the 1922 political hubbub of Rome where he would soon learn an ex-Socialist journalist turned Fascist spokesman successfully made a bid for power that before long would prove absolute. All at once Cosimu was thirty-four, a novice in a new time and place. Fortunately now he was under the protective wing of Roberto Donatelli.

Still, he found himself disoriented in an expressway life that daily hurtled him forward, finally delivering him the fortune of prominence on the coattails of Mussolini himself, who came to regard Lipani as "the one Sicilian I would trust with my life."

And life was good, Attendant Marcu. Il Duce——our Leader!—took us through the decades of the 20s and 30s where we his ministers reaped the fruits of conquest. Recipients of a new world order. The hero of all Italy had promised the Italian people, and was delivering, a final Roman Empire, one that this time would survive. Once more Italy could wave its colors. Even in Africa, because of fascism, the cannibals stopped devouring one another and began studying at the university! Mussolini had lifted Italy out of the doldrums of a history that had neglected her for too many centuries. Only the delinquents hated him—especially *li mafiusi siciliani*, those Sicilian gangsters forced to guzzle Il Duce's castor oil for infractions against the Italian state.

Can you fathom such a world, Marcu? You back here in 1900? Why, not even Mussolini, a seventeen-year-old somewhere in a town called Predappio in northern Italy's Romagna, could in his wildest dreams suspect one day he will change the face of Italy!

Cosimu flinched when he felt Marcu's hand adjust the cloak around Cosimu's stooped shoulders. It jolted him back to the moment, back to the madhouse some lied and called the sanitarium.

"Signur' Ministru, or better still, *Signur' Misteriu*—Mr. Mystery Man! Three months here and perhaps today, at last, we shall open some locked doors. What do you say? A visitor is waiting for you. Who might that be? In your ranting delirium those first few days here you cried like a schoolboy. 'Carmelu and Teresa Lipani, my parents in Acquaviva Platani, the province of Caltanissetta. Bring them here. They will tell you who I am.'"

But when the young couple arrived, they wept to see a fifty-six year old derelict named Cosimu Lipani, a madman on his knees, begging this couple much younger than himself, to take him home. *"Sugnu tò figghiu. Sugnu Cosimu Lipani. Salvatemi!"* ['I am your son. I am Cosimu Lipani. Save me!']

"You cried like a boy and thank God you frightened them away! Cosimu. Like their missing son. Cosimu Lipani, no less. But it was not their son. *'Diu Miu! Ma, chi fai—scherzi?'* ['My God! What are you doing—playing games?'] Their little Cosimu still trapped inside that cursed salt mine. Instead, you present yourself to them, a slap in the face, a cruel prank, even for a madman, Sir.

"Three months ago. Your first two visitors. Today," said Marcu, "another visitor comes. Will you speak again?"

Recalling that pitiful encounter, Cosimu brushed tears from both eyes. He had seen his parents again after forty-four years. Saw them young as when he had left them that Saturday morning— only two weeks before!—when he himself was twelve-years-young and so foolish. It broke his heart! Now someone else has come. No, Marcu, I will never speak again. Send the visitor away or bring the visitor to me. Either way it cannot matter anymore.

Cosimu let his mind go back to where and when he had left off...

Remembering his past was a daily exercise in self-reproach: heavy penance for his crimes. Blindly he had followed the leader. He had traded the Christ of his childhood for this new divinity who had gone from well-meaning to maniacal, from calling himself Il Duce, the Leader of Italy, to calling himself Italy itself!

Mussolini had hitched his destiny to that of Germany's Hitler, so together they could conquer the world. Il Duce, despite his boasting how he knew what was best for Italy, was in reality quite naive to think he could fall under the Nazi spell and not become enslaved. In the end, mistaking Hitler's aggression for concern, he had welcomed the goose-stepping German military hoards to occupy Italy. Earlier he had even followed Hitler's lead and deported Italian Jews out of Italy. In cattle cars. To death camps.

By order of King Victor Emmanuel III, Mussolini was arrested on July 25, 1943. Marshal Pietro Badoglio, his former Army Chief-of-Staff, took over as head of the new Italian government. Four days later, Mussolini spent his sixtieth birthday in a cell. On September 23 of that year, he returned to power. Hitler had sent parachutists to rescue him.

In January, while a world war raged, so did Mussolini's hunger for revenge. So did the executions. Socialist enemies of the old days, Fascist ministers less than totally loyal, high-ranking military officers, finally even Mussolini's son-in-law, Minister Galeazzo Ciano! Fascist traitors strapped in wooden chairs, like cowards, were shot in the back.

Cosimu recalled those days. Anyone suspected of treason was hunted down and murdered. Only two years before, Mussolini had replaced the old Secret Police Chief, Renzo Chierici, with his trusted ally from the early days, Roberto Donatelli. He could count on him to efficiently dispatch those who would dare treason against him, against fascism, against Italy itself. Mussolini, a man of letters with a penchant for irony, appointed Donatelli, a man with an iron hand, someone brutal as he. In hiding, Mussolini could rest assured Donatelli would be unrelenting in his disposal of Il Duce's enemies.

Even Cosimu himself, the Sicilian whom Mussolini trusted, was not above suspicion. Italo Rossi, brother of Cosimu's late wife Lisabetta, had been arrested for clandestine activities against the state. He had joined the partisans who had vowed to kill Benito Mussolini.

When Rossi was shot in a pretense of resisting arrest, Cosimu fled. He had fallen out of favor; he had seen and said too much. Donatelli, once his mentor, had grown vicious with power and had taken Mussolini's words to heart: "If I go forward, follow me; if I go backward, kill me; if I die, avenge me." Mussolini, very much alive, now had enemies everywhere. The partisans who regarded Mussolini as a traitor to Italy, a dictator who had gone backwards and by his own words had asked for death, were committed to hold him to his word. Cosimu stood in the midst of both sides.

Deep under the Church of Mary Magdalene where once the early Christians hid from persecution, Cosimu Lipani harbored no illusions God would save him. He sat huddled in the corner of the dark catacombed cell, staring at the labyrinth of stone passageways in a sinuous tunnel of stone that could perhaps lead to freedom. No, not to freedom. To judgment, he decided. To judgment. Cosimu clasped his eyes shut and held his breath. If he could have had his own way, he would've willed his own death, but instead, like a trapped rat he pushed himself through the mazed darkness, playing one stone passageway against the next in a shell game of survival, a game he was certain he could not win. Finding it oppressive to breathe the chalky air so far beneath the Roman city, he toyed with the notion of sitting down and admitting defeat, but he had come this far, so he stepped through one last archway of stone.

Sunlight blinded him. He heard voices, and for the second time since a lifetime ago, he was falling skyward like film spooling in reverse; like a fool walking his life backwards in a futile last-ditch effort to undo sin and stupidity; like time playing everything back to the alpha where it all began.

It was the last act to a tragic life he was hopefully leaving behind, but then God added His own comedic finish: He returned Cosimu Lipani to Sicily. About a half a mile from the madhouse in Palermo. In the same year he had left Sicily: 1900, two weeks after he had vanished as a boy. February. Mid-afternoon. But he wasn't twelve again. That would've been too kind, he knew, and surely not what he deserved.

Still, there was the matter of Benito Mussolini, one of at least two Anti-Christs plaguing the century, this future modern-day Nero who would not rest until he obliterated all of Italy and Sicily in a sweep of doomsday fire. He had to warn Italy, veer the country from this collision course with an ill-fated history no one in 1900 could even wildly foresee. He alone—Cosimu Lipani—had been thrust into the future and had seen with his own eyes the mark of the beast in John's Revelation.

And too there was the matter of his henchman—the other iron hand: Donatelli. He remembered the moral to the fairy tale his grandmother had recounted: *"Cu priparala fossa pi l'autri, ci caddi iddu stissu nilla fossa."* ["Who prepares the pit for others, will himself fall into it.."]

Cosimu knew what had to be done. It was the start of a new century. He would go to northern Italy, to that little town of Predappio and kill the young Mussolini and in so doing save the world. At least he wished he could, but who in his right mind would trust a loaded pistol in the hand of a seeming madman?

He sat huddled on the cobblestone curb, trembling in the light of impending judgment. He clamped his eyes shut and for a moment held his breath. He would've willed his own death, if he could have done so, but instead, like a spoiled boy, he kicked out his legs and thrashed his arms, cried for his parents, for his boyhood Friends—Sarbaturi, Vannu,

Antò—sleeping peacefully in their beds. But when the Palermo *Polizia* arrived, there was no fight left in him. He settled himself into a quiet surrender.

"Sigur' Lipani," Marcu called from the other end of the sitting room. "Your visitor is here." Cosimu nodded. "This way, Signur'," he heard Marcu say. "Signur' Ministru…" Marcu covered his mouth and laughed into his hand. "No disrespect, of course. It is the name he gave himself when first he came to us. *"Sugnu nu ministru di lu statu!"* ["I am a minister of state'] Signur', here in this sanitarium we have many such dignitaries. Over in that corner there, across from Signur' Lipani sits Signur' Julius Caesar. The fellow addresses us all as 'Brutus.' He believes this sitting room is the Roman Senate!"

Cosimu Lipani shivered as the cold weight pressed against his collarbone, fingers curving in an easy vise. He turned his head sideways, training his dark eyes downward where he saw his own reflection—a dead man's—in the mirrored surface of Donatelli's iron hand.

AFTERWARD

This second printing of *A Family of Sicilians: Stories and Poems* celebrates the tenth anniversary of its first publication back in 1998. How the years flew by! In 1998, New York's skyline still boasted the beauty of The Twin Towers at New York City's World Trade Center, fanatic terrorism had not yet so boldly threatened our security, and America was preparing to close the millennium with an optimistic eye to the start of a new century. All that changed one horrific September 11th Tuesday morning in 2001. The nation is still experiencing the after-shocks of that tragic event.

Originally I had written this book to demonstrate my pride in being the son of a Sicilian and a Sicilian American. In 1965, after being graduated from Seton Hall University, I spent a glorious year in the little mountain village from which my parents came: Acquaviva Platani! It was a dream fulfilled, one I knew needed telling. I still remember my cousin Padre Alfonso Giannino asking me back then as we walked together up and down the cobblestone streets of that old *paisi,* "And what will become of these notebook scribblings of yours,

190

Salvatore? Will all these observations one day find a home in a book or in a wastebasket?"

I also wrote this book to show a truer image of Sicilians and Sicilian Americans in order to combat the prejudiced stereotypes foisted on us by the media. Ten years later, the media continues to badmouth my ethnic group, so the battle goes on.

The sale of the complete first-run printing of 1,000 copies was a pleasant surprise, and so were the many subsequent orders I could not fill. Perhaps now I will be able to do so.

I thank my friends Tovli and Yosif Simiryan for making this second printing possible. I also thank my long-time friend Anthony Buccino for his help and encouragement. And I thank all of you who read my book. But first and foremost, I thank my wife Sharon for loving me and for understanding my need to write.

ABOUT THE AUTHOR

SALVATORE AMICO M. BUTTACI was born in New York in 1941, attended Seton Hall University and Rutgers Graduate School of Management. A retired teacher, he taught English in New Jersey at a local middle school and at a community college. Many of his poems, stories, letters, and articles have been published here and abroad in such publications as *The New York Times*, *U.S.A. Today*, *The Writer*, and *Christian Science Monitor*. Recently he completed a collection of his poems, *A Dusting of Star Fall: Love Poems*, as well as a two-volume bilingual book of Sicilian proverbs called *Comu Dissu Iddu / As He Said.*

In 2006, he was the recipient of the Cyber-wit $500.00 Poetry Award for Poetry.

The former editor of New Worlds Unlimited (1974-1988), Buttaci is currently Editor of The Poem Factory on the Internet. Visit him at his sites: http://www.freewebs.com/sambpoet and at http://www.geocities.com/sambpoet. He also writes a column called "Poet Craft" in *Poetidings*, the newsletter of the New Jersey Poetry Society, Inc., of which he is a long-standing member. He is also a member of the West Virginia Writers and Poets Group at http://www.writerscafe.org.

The author lives in West Virginia, with his wife, the love of his life, Sharon.

PRAISE FOR A FAMILY OF SICILIANS...

"Woven throughout Buttaci's stories and poems is the rich tenderness that Sicilians should be known for. This is the book that no Italian-American should be without. Thank you, Mr. Buttaci, for setting the record straight."

—Erin L. Wright, Editor-In-Chief, *Buon Giorgno! Magazine*, Columbus, Ohio

"These stories and poems are testimony to Buttaci's ability as poet and storyteller and will certainly delight all readers, especially those of Sicilian heritage." —Anne Marie Giovingo, Assistant Editor, *Italian-American Digest*, New Orleans, LA

"Reading *A Family of Sicilians...* brings me back to a happy nostaligic time spent with Nonna Montagnino, my maternal grandmother from Mussomeli, Sicily!"

—Robert R. Scussel, Past President, local chapter of UNICO NATIONAL, Garfield, NJ

"Your work is wonderful! You really have the soul of Sicily in the book. You have living portraits of life in Sicily. I've never read anything so forceful about Sicily. Really, when you start reading, you do not stop; you want to go to the end and no page tires you out. All told, your work brims with life on every page. With your trips to

Sicily, you hot hold of its soul, mind, heart. All my heartfelt congratulations, Professor Buttaci. God bless you!"

—Professor Antonio Ciappina, Secretary-Treasurer of *America Oggi*, Westwood, NJ

"You don't have to be Sicilian or even Italian to appreciate the warmth, humor, and love of family and life, portrayed by Salvatore Amico M. Buttaci in his book *A Family of Sicilians...*"

—Herb Berman, Publisher of *VIA: The Voice of the Italian-American*, Tamarac, FL

"Buttaci's new publication *A Family of Sicilians: Stories and Poems* has received excellent response in North Jersey. More than 100 people turned out at Good Fellas Restaurant in Garfield, NJ, for his book signing."

—Rosalie Longo, *Herald News*, Passaic, NJ

"Its passages evoke the same kind of insightful images of character and locale found in the best of Umberto Eco and Italy's most passionate novelist and short story writer Alberto Moravia. It's the characters found in Buttaci's prose that are truly the voice of immigrants, their hopes and their aspirations."

—A. J. Parisi, *Village Gazette of Ridgewood*, Franklin Lakes, NJ

Also by Salvatore Amico M. Buttaci
A DUSTING OF STAR FALL: LOVE POEMS

"Sal Amico M. Buttaci, teacher, instructor, writer, and poet, has given us a gift to cherish. These poems, written for the poet's wife Sharon, contain a message for all of us in describing the fulfillment of a very human yearning— the desire to express love, to cherish the beloved, and, in return, to be cherished. It is a book written for all of us! The love poems in this delightful book speak to our inmost feelings, and for that, his readers will be exceedingly thankful.

With the wisdom of a long-time teacher, this poet urges us in his poems to find and keep that one essential quality: the giving and sharing of love that can accompany us through life and render us partners in a sublime world of our own making."

—Moira Bailis, New Jersey poet and radio host

This collection of the author's recently published poems is a 142-page book, published by Cyber-wit Publications in India, soft cover, perfect-bound. ISBN: 81-8253-054-7.

$15.00 plus $3.00 handling and shipping. Send check to Salvatore Buttaci, 709 Straley Avenue, Apt. 4, Princeton, West Virginia 24740.